CASH, CARS, & KISSES

Also by John Fulker

And True Deliverance Make (1985)
The View From Above (1992)
Chicken Soup, Cheap Whiskey & Bad Women (2000)
Shards & Pellets & Knives, Oh My! (2007)

CASH, CARS, & KISSES

Another Murder Trilogy

John Fulker

ORANGE *frazer* PRESS
Wilmington, Ohio

ISBN 978-1933197968

Published for John Edward Fulker by:
Orange Frazer Press
P.O. Box 214
Wilmington, OH 45177
Telephone: 800.852.9332 for price and shipping information.
Website: www.orangefrazer.com
www.orangefrazercustombooks.com

Cover illustrations and book illustrations by Meryl Sklut-Lettire
Book and cover design: Brittany Lament and Orange Frazer Press

Library of Congress Control Number 2012938085

And yet another, for NJ

CASH, CARS, & KISSES

CASH

Part One

1

Bud Hughes didn't really amount to a tinker's dam—never had, and, in a larger sense, never would. He had dropped out of school at age sixteen, the minimum allowed by law. Although it was certain that he had never entered high school, no one could have said what academic level he had attained before he quit altogether. Because of his total inattention to both his studies and the required classroom decorum, he was, early on, consigned to what was then called the "ungraded room"—or, more colloquially, the "dummy room." At recess, he seldom tossed a football, played softball, shot baskets, or engaged in any of the usual pursuits common to grade school kids. His preferred school-ground activities consisted principally of bullying or otherwise harassing the younger boys, annoying the girls and flipping off the teachers. His favorite pastime was to loiter near the upright drinking fountain and, at the opportune moment, to forcibly shove the head of a thirst-quenching student downward onto the spigot. It was a major coup for him if the student bled at the mouth or lost a tooth as a result.

It wasn't so much that he was stupid, or mentally impaired, or even vicious. He just didn't care—about anything. Born in 1925, he had grown up in the small town of Troy, Ohio, during the Great Depression, the product of a broken home, and was seemingly doomed by circumstance and by his own total lack of motivation to slog his way through an essentially unproductive and feckless existence.

In appearance, he was not unattractive. Slightly above average height, perhaps five-feet ten or eleven, he was lean and, while certainly not athletic, he seemed reasonably fit. With regular features, straight dark hair, and a predilection for black or blue clothing, jeans and jackets, he looked as though he might have invented himself in Elvis Presley's image years before the latter's meteoric rise to prominence.

In the years after he had left school, he performed—or pulled—the occasional odd job in order to supplement that which he was able to wheedle from either his mother or one of her consorts in order to finance his growing addiction to alcohol. By the time he was thirty, he had become a confirmed alcoholic, petty thief, and when he could get away with it, a forger and sometime grifter. He was well known to the local authorities and had spent a very considerable part of his young life in the local Miami County jail. Paradoxically, however, he did exude a kind of risqué charm and was considered by many who knew him to be something of a "player."

In 1954, Christmas fell on a Saturday, and though Bud Hughes had never celebrated the holiday season in traditional ways, he nonetheless welcomed the event as a good reason to drink and carouse, either in solitude or in the company of one or another of his few friends and acquaintances. As it happens, he had begun to drink heavily on Friday, Christmas Eve, and had kept at it throughout the holidays. By Monday, the twenty-seventh, he'd been unable to rouse himself until early evening. He got a bit of assistance in that endeavor by the arrival of one of his drinking buddies, Jim Abshire from nearby Piqua. Abshire hadn't bothered to knock; he simply barged into the small bungalow where Bud lived with his mother. He found his friend seated, head in hands and rubbing his eyes, on the worn naugahyde couch in the barren front room. "Hey, Bud," he greeted. "Wanna grab a beer?"

Then, without waiting for an answer, he commented, "Jesus! Maybe you ain't up to it tonight—you look like shit warmed over! Too much holiday?"

Bud struggled to his feet like an arthritic old man whose joints had taken an uncomfortable set, cleared his throat of an unsettling accumulation of phlegm, and groaned audibly.

"Yeah? Well you don't look all that great either. Hell, I'm all right. The holidays don't have much effect on me; I don't do any of that yuletide crap. And I sure don't do any Christmas shopping. Haven't bought anybody a gift in years. Come to think of it, nobody's bought me one either, so I guess it evens out." He indulged himself in a long, lethargic stretch, stifled a yawn and added, "Actually, I figured out some time back that there ain't no Santa Claus." He looked quizzically at Abshire and asked, "Did you know that? There just ain't no fucking Santa Claus."

Abshire grimaced at the remark. "Yeah," he agreed, "I'd kinda worked that out for myself. You wanna get a beer or not?" And before the answer came, he added, "You remember Eddie McMullen? You should, he's about your age. Went to high school here a coupla years back, played some baseball, then quit school 'bout the same time you did—at sixteen—went to work driving a truck for Ray Hawley, then worked awhile for Trojan Coal 'till his old man moved them all back to Greenfield. Remember him?"

Bud Hughes scratched his head, then acknowledged, "Oh, yeah. I know who you mean. What'd he do?"

"He didn't *do* anything, you moron," answered Abshire. "He's outside in his car; he drove me here to see if you wanted to get a beer. Do you, or not?"

"Why the hell didn't you say so in the first place? Of course I want a beer. I'm dry as dust. Besides, I need something for the headache I got last night. Where we going?"

Thus satisfied, Bud needed only a moment to change his shirt and run a comb through his hair. Then, after he and Abshire were comfortably ensconced in McMullen's small car and en route to Troy's Orchard Tavern, Bud and Eddie McMullen re-acquainted themselves with one another. It soon became apparent that both Hughes and Abshire had already spent most of the weekend partaking of the several hairs of the respective dogs that had repeatedly bitten them most of their waking hours. By the time they'd ingested "a coupla beers" at the Orchard Tavern north of town, another couple at the Idle Hour downtown, and a pair of boiler-makers at Walt's Tavern south of town, they were both pretty well wasted. Eddie McMullen had kept pace with them, but the fact that they'd had a head start on him soon became obvious.

Although they'd really had very little history together, their conversation consisted mainly of catching one another up on their respective antics and activities over the ten or twelve years since they had last seen one another. By the time they had exhausted that subject, Jim Abshire had noticed the .38

caliber revolver protruding from under McMullen's belt; he was especially impressed by its flashy pearl handle. "Nice grips, Eddie," he pronounced. "How'd you come by that?"

"Never mind where I got it," McMullen bruited. "What's important is that I've got it where I can get to it when I need it."

And, almost in linear fashion, their conversation ultimately took them to some of the locally recognized opportunities for a quick score. Eddie McMullen seemed to be intrigued upon learning of an old man named Chipley, who was supposed to operate a used furniture store in an outbuilding located just outside his home on Madison Avenue. The store was open for business virtually anytime Chipley was at home and awake. He was also reputed to carry large amounts of cash on his person.

"A used furniture store, you say?" he inquired of Bud Hughes.

"That's right," said Hughes. "He retired from Troy Sunshade six or seven years ago and started to deal in used furniture. Not antiques or anything like that. Just used. But," he added, "he does seem to make a lotta' money out of it."

"Well, now," mused McMullen aloud. "That's a happy coincidence. Me and my wife have been looking for a small used stove; wonder if he might have one. It's only a little after nine o'clock. Maybe we could go see what he's got."

It was a short trip from Walt's Tavern to Madison Avenue. They didn't need an address. Bud Hughes knew the place well; it was located within a few blocks of his own home. By the time they arrived at the Chipley residence, however, both Hughes and Abshire were stretched out in the back seat of McMullen's car, blithely drinking themselves into a stupor. McMullen drove past the house, noted that it was well lighted, and proceeded on past it. He turned right at the next intersection, onto Jefferson Street, and coasted to a stop at the curb.

"Not here, Dipshit," cried Hughes. "You just passed it on Madison."

"No matter," said McMullen. "I can walk back. You guys stay here; I'll just see what he's got. Be right back. Save me some of that hootch, will ya?" And with that, he slipped out of the driver's seat, slammed the door and made his way around the corner towards the Chipley home.

No more than a few minutes later, Bud Hughes and Jim Abshire's alcohol-induced reveries were interrupted by the dull sound of nearby gunshots, and within another minute Eddie McMullen was back; he'd run from the rear of the Chipley home, down an alleyway and onto Jefferson. As he jumped into the car, his companions noted that one or more of his fingers were bleeding profusely. When asked about it, he simply grunted that he'd had an accident. Then, with no further ado, he quickly started the engine and announced that he had to be back in Greenfield by eleven o'clock. From Jefferson Street, he drove, at breakneck speeds, the ten or twelve blocks to the intersection of Water and Market Streets, where he unceremoniously dumped his two passengers and headed out of town. "Gotta run," he shouted back at them as soon as their feet had hit the pavement. "Promised my wife I'd be home by 'leven. See you guys next time."

Some two hours later Bud Hughes found himself in yet another local bar where he learned, for the first time, that Grover Cleveland Chipley, aged sixty-nine, had been robbed and murdered.

2

Eddie McMullen's hasty departure from the city of Troy coincided almost precisely with the arrival of police officers Virgil Cruea and Jack Cheadle at the Chipley residence. They had been on patrol, cruising in the general vicinity when summoned by radio. Headquarters radioed to tell them about an urgent telephone call from Cleve Chipley's sister, Kathryn Leffel, and the two officers were on the scene by 9:18, just three minutes after receiving the call.

They found Chipley lying on his back on the floor of the concrete block building located just behind his home, the back of his head wedged into the corner. He was still alive, but unconscious and bleeding from apparent gunshot wounds to his left shoulder, stomach and thumb. Patrolman Cheadle took in the scene at a glance and immediately radioed for an ambulance.

"I've already telephoned," assured Kathryn Leffel. "Actually, I made that call before I called you people. I had really expected them to be here by now."

"I'm sure you did," Cheadle assured her. "Sometimes we get a quicker response than you will—because they know it's a police matter." And with that, he proceeded to the front of the residence to meet the incoming ambulance and guide the driver through the alley alongside the house to the block building at the rear. Cheadle's next call was to Police Chief John Hennessey, whom he found at home. Hennessey arrived, by taxicab, within minutes and immediately joined his officers in their investigations.

Just before the Chief's arrival and while Cheadle was in process of assisting the ambulance attendants transfer the injured Chipley into their vehicle, Patrolman Cruea had begun a cursory examination of the premises, made a few preliminary notes and sketches, and cautioned each member of the small crew that had gathered that none of them should leave the scene until they had been properly identified and interviewed.

He also radioed police headquarters to report what little information they'd come by thus far, and then—based on a rudimentary description of the suspected assailant and believing him to have fled by automobile—he telephoned the two local taxicab companies, all of the dozen or so local gas stations, and the police departments of surrounding communities and asked them to be on the look-out for suspicious persons; he also alerted the district headquarters of the state highway patrol at nearby Wilmington, Ohio, with the same request. He later learned that road blocks had been established at all of the major roads in the area—all, of course, to no avail.

Finally, after the ambulance had left for the hospital, Chief Hennessey and Officers Cheadle and Cruea jointly identified and "statementized" all those in attendance. They needed to learn what had happened, the "how, who, what, when and where" information with which to create a file and to begin their investigation.

Della Chipley, the wife of Cleve Chipley told the officers that she and her husband were enjoying a quiet evening at home; they'd had family in at the time. At approximately eight

Chief John Hennessey

o'clock her brother, Robert Leffel, his wife, Kathryn, their son and daughter-in-law, William and Patricia Leffel, had stopped by for a visit. Then, shortly after nine, the doorbell rang and she answered it to find a stranger who said he wanted her husband to show him a stove. She said she hadn't gotten a good look at him because he had remained outside in the dark. She went to her husband, gave him the information and asked him not to go. "It's late—it's dark—and it's still holiday time. Who goes shopping at a used furniture store after nine o'clock at night just two days after Christmas? We don't know this person from Adam's off-ox. I don't like it and I think you should tell him to come back tomorrow—during the daytime." However, despite her remonstrances, her husband went outside, spoke with the man and arranged to meet him at his shop behind the house.

The stranger went through the alley to the store and her husband donned a light jacket, pocketed his .32 caliber pistol, and walked out the back door to the store. "Because I was nervous about it," she said tearfully, "I asked Robert and William to come along, and the three of us followed along towards the store. We were about half-way there when we heard three shots fired. I froze in my tracks, but Robert and William apparently realized what had happened and they ran back to the house to call an ambulance. I heard my husband call my name and call for help, so I ran to him and found him on the floor at the far end of the store; by the time I got to him he was already unconscious and he was soaked in blood. I didn't see the stranger again; he just seemed to have disappeared."

While Della was making her statement, twenty-two-year-old William Leffel returned to the house. He told Cheadle that he was Cleve Chipley's nephew, home on leave from army duty at Fort Belvoir, Virginia, and was visiting his aunt and uncle in company with his parents. He confirmed all that his aunt Della had reported and added that as he and his father were running towards the house to summon help, he had looked back towards the store and seen the stranger outside the east doorway of the store. "He just stood there for a second or two, then turned and ran down the alley. He looked directly at me for a moment, but I didn't get a real good look at him because it was raining and the alley light was out. The lights inside the store were on, though, and I could see him well enough to tell that he was wearing tan-colored clothes—like khaki—pants and windbreaker. He was fairly tall, maybe five-feet seven or eight inches, perhaps more, and he was lean, probably in his early thirties—and he had sandy hair, all messed up. I remember calling to my father, 'There he goes!' My mom called for an ambulance and for the police, and I got my truck and drove around the neighborhood in hopes I might catch some sight of the guy—or maybe a vehicle and I could get a license plate. I got close to Zwiebel's corner just as the ambulance went by, my father with it, so I came back here; I didn't want my aunt and my mom to be here alone."

He looked around the crowded room and added, "I guess they're not alone now, but I need to be here anyway."

All of the family members acknowledged that Chipley was generally known to have carried large amounts of cash on his person. Then the interviews were interrupted by a telephone message advising that Cleve Chipley had died en route to the hospital. He was pronounced dead on arrival and his body submitted to Dr. William Adkins, the Miami County coroner, for examination.

During a further search of the store premises that same evening, the police officers found a trail of blood, from which they inferred that Chipley had been shot near the large overhead door at the center of the building and that he had then chased his attacker towards the east door through which he had been seen to escape. They also found an old .32 caliber, nickel-plated revolver on the floor near his head. That weapon was identified by Della Chipley as her husband's gun. They found a live shell, with an indentation from an apparent hammer strike, in the chamber, and two others on the floor near the beginning of the blood trail. Chief Hennessey noted that the gun was an old one and theorized that Chipley had attempted to fire it at his assailant, but the shell had failed to detonate; he also guessed that the shells found on the floor had simply fallen out of the gun. He reloaded the weapon and demonstrated that when the gun was elevated the shells would simply fall out of the worn cylinder.

Later that same evening, Coroner Adkins reported that his examination indicated that Chipley had sustained four wounds, one to his left shoulder, two to his stomach and one to his thumb. He theorized that he had been shot three times, but that one of the bullets had passed through his thumb before striking a more vital area. He also recovered two bullets that had apparently passed through his body and come to rest in his clothing. The bullets were turned over to Chief Hennessey for safekeeping.

3

Not surprisingly, Eddie McMullen made good time on his return trip to Greenfield. By the same token, he had paid assiduous attention to his driving. He sure-Lord couldn't afford a traffic stop. He'd had way too much to drink, blood on his clothing, Cleve Chipley's wallet in his pocket and a pearl-handled .38, with three spent shells in the cylinder and the distinctive odor of detonated gunpowder, tucked in his belt. He also felt an abiding confidence that the law enforcement people would be on the lookout for anything out of the ordinary. What needed to happen, he realized, was that he put all the miles he could between himself and the city of Troy as quickly as possible without attracting attention.

He managed to accomplish the trip without incident and arrived in Greenfield shortly after 11:00 that night. Having cleared that significant hurdle, his confidence soared. He was home free.

Nonetheless, he realized that he still had some "house keeping" chores to tend to before he could call it a day. First on his list was to return the snub-nosed, pearl-handled .38 revolver he had borrowed earlier that same day from his good friend and drinking buddy, Cecil Maddy. And to that end, he drove straight to the Maddy residence just a mile or so out of town. To his dismay, and despite the late hour, he found neither Cecil, nor Ella Mae, his wife, at home. Their 17 year-old son, Cecil Lee Maddy, was the only person there. "I think Dad's still pouring drinks at Ada's. Mom's probably there too, but I can't promise you that," he said.

"I figured he'd have shut down before now," Eddie remarked casually. "I'll find him."

He climbed into his car and headed back to the center of town where Ada's Bar was prominently located—and where Cecil Maddy was the manager, the barkeep and also, because of his devil-may-care persona, the principal attraction. Another popular watering hole, located in the same neighborhood, was "Maddy's Smoke Shop", a card-playing establishment, just a few doors removed from Ada's. The sometime manager of that establishment was another of Eddie's close friends, Glen Purdin, who also worked part-time at Ada's for Cecil Maddy. Rather than proceeding directly to Ada's, Eddie stopped by the Smoke Shop, found Purdin, surreptitiously slipped him the revolver and asked him to give it to Maddy.

"By the way," Eddie said as Maddy slid the gun under his belt, "that check for $38 I gave you this morning to cover my poker loss—you still got it?"

"Yeah, I got it," Purdin answered. "Been too busy to get to the bank. Why? You want it back?"

"Matter of fact, I do," said Eddie. "Seems I just came into a little money. I'll buy it back from you. Save you that trip to the bank." And he peeled a fifty-dollar bill from the roll of bills he extracted from his pocket and offered it to Purdy.

"Damn! That's some wad you're sportin'; I guess you did come into some money. Wha'd'ya do, rob a bank?" he asked. He waved the fifty-dollar bill back at Eddie. "I ain't got change for that."

By way of response, Eddie flashed a poorly disguised smirk and winked, "Hell, no, man. I didn't rob no bank. And I don't need change for the fifty. You keep it." He stuffed the remaining bills back in his pocket. "You go on over to Ada's now and give the rod to Maddy, okay? I may see you there later."

Purdin shoved the revolver into his belt, closed his shirt over it and left on his errand. Eddie McMullen remained at the Smoke Shop and swigged two beers between gritted teeth; his injured finger had begun to throb. Then, after what he considered an appropriate interval, he moved on to Ada's. By that time, his finger was really hurting; maybe, he decided, he needed something stronger—and perhaps a bit of stimulating company, too.

As late as it was, Ada's Bar was still exceptionally crowded that evening and, for that reason Glen Purdin, who had already delivered the revolver to Cecil Maddy, hadn't seen Eddie McMullen come into the bar some twenty minutes later. When he finally did notice him, it was at a time when Cecil Maddy and another friend, Nick Valentine, were making a spectacle of buying drinks for the house. Purdin threw his arm around Eddie's shoulder and waltzed him out onto the street, ostensibly to drive him to Club 28, another honky-tonk located just west of Greenfield. The real reason for his intervention was, of course, to prevent him from joining in the general hilarity, and provoking curiosity as to just exactly what it was Maddy and Valentine were celebrating and what the source of their newly acquired affluence might have been.

"You've been actin' kinda strange, and you ain't lookin' so hot either. You've got bloodstains on your clothes and you've obviously hurt your hand somehow—and you had me give Cecil that pearl-handled revolver. I don't know what's up with you," he told Eddie as they drove the mile or so to Club 28. "And I don't know where you got that wad of cash you're flashin'—either you or Cecil—or Valentine, either," he said, and then quickly added, "And, I don't wanna know, okay? Don't tell me nuthin'. What's more," he admonished, "you'd be best advised to keep that wad in your pocket and your mouth shut."

"You're right, Glen," Eddie acknowledged as they sat in Purdin's car outside Club 28. "Take me back to Ada's; give me a minute with Maddy, and I'll go home to bed, okay?"

"Promise?"

"Yeah, I promise. I need to be more careful. 'Sides, I'm tired and my finger hurts like hell."

Purdin shot a quick glance at Eddie's finger. "I already noticed you got it chewed up pretty good. You get in an argument with a pissed-off racoon?"

"Not hardly," came the too-quick reply. "I slammed my car door on it; I oughta pay more attention to what I'm doin'."

"That's true enough," said Purdin. "Seems to me you do need to watch what you're doin'—and what you're sayin' to people, too. Best place for you is in bed. Things'll look different in the morning."

With that final admonition, and without ever entering Club 28, Purdin re-engaged the clutch, dropped Eddie off at Ada's and drove on home to his apartment above the Smoke Shop.

Eddie went directly to the back room at Ada's bar and found Cecil Maddy at his desk, checking the daily receipts and preparing an inventory list with which to restock the bar for the balance of the week. The two men had barely had a chance to acknowledge one another when Cecil's wife, Ella Mae, entered from the inside doorway. Both of the Maddys remarked about what appeared to be bloodstains on Eddie's light tan air force jacket and on the side of his khaki pants. "What did you do, Eddie? Did you hurt someone?" Cecil asked.

"Well, yeah, kinda," answered Eddie McMullen with a touch of forced bravado. "The son-of-a-bitch pulled a rod on me, and..." He stammered for a moment and then finished with, "but I don't think he'll be able to pull it on anybody else."

Cecil Maddy looked to his wife, "Ella Mae, you go on out front. Let me try to get this dumb bastard cleaned up. We'll come out after a bit."

Ella Mae did as she was told and some 45 minutes later the two men joined her. Eddie was wearing a different pair of pants and a shirt that she recognized as one of Cecil's. His injured finger had been bandaged, but he still looked pale and shaky.

"Yeah, yeah," acknowledged Cecil when Ella Mae raised a questioning eyebrow. "I took him home, cleaned him up as best I could and got him into some of my clothes; we're about the same size. I even bandaged his finger, but he's gonna need to see a doctor about that tomorrow."

"Where were the kids while you were putting Eddie back together?" asked Ella Mae.

"Both in bed," Cecil assured her. "Cecil Lee got up to go to the bathroom and heard us messin' around, but I sent him back to bed."

What Cecil didn't know was that while in the bathroom, Cecil Lee had seen a khaki air force jacket and an old, dark billfold on the floor. He checked out the billfold and noted that it contained no cash. It did, however, contain a driver's license in the name of Cleveland Chipley. He left both items where he'd found them and turned back towards his bedroom. As he passed his father's room, he happened to see his father's distinctive pearl-handled revolver lying on the bed, and, upon closer examination, he noted that it contained three spent shell casings and three unfired shells in the cylinder. He had known better than to make any inquiries and so went back to bed.

Cleaned up and in his borrowed clothing Eddie McMullen stood with Cecil Maddy at the bar near a stool where Ella Mae had taken up station on a barstool beside her friend Dorothy Newland. With Eddie plainly in tow, Maddy pushed his way up to the bar and threw out a hefty roll of bills. "Set 'em up for everybody," he told the bartender. "We got a real live hero here with us tonight. We got things to celebrate."

Then he felt a firm grip on his shoulder and Glen Purdin, whom everyone thought had gone to bed for the night, re-appeared. "Put the money away, Cece," he said quietly. "You're worse than Eddie. Just put it away and get hold of yourself." Maddy hesitated a moment, then scooped up the roll of bills and stuffed them into his shirt-pocket. "Gotcha," he said. "You're right."

The small coterie of friends, now joined by Nick Valentine, remained at the bar, talking quietly among themselves, for another hour or so until 2:30 a.m., closing time. Then Maddy told Ella Mae to go on home. "We'll be along in a minute," he said. "I've got to close up first. I'll bring Eddie with me. He can stay the night with us."

"Alright, Cecil, whatever you say," she answered meekly. And with that, she, along with Dorothy Newland and Nick Valentine, drove to her home and awaited her husband's arrival.

The three of them sat in the living room, making small talk—killing time—for no more than a few minutes before they heard Cecil and Eddie come into the kitchen. Ella Mae left her two friends and entered the kitchen where she found the two men sitting at the table. Because she assumed they were hungry, she warmed up the fried chicken and mashed potatoes she had prepared for Cecil earlier in the evening. While engaged in that task, she overheard Cecil ask Eddie, "How strong did you go?"

When she heard no answer, she looked at Eddie; he simply dropped his head and remained silent. By that time, he was too sick to eat and got up to go to bed. "Where can I sleep?" he asked plaintively.

Maddy looked to his wife with grim resignation and sighed, "Put him in our room; we'll make do for the night. But I want him outa here in the morning." Then, before Ella Mae could help Eddie to their room, Cecil growled, "One more thing," he added. "Burn his goddamn clothes—all of them. You hear? Every stitch. He can wear some of my stuff till he gets home in the morning."

Eddie McMullen tried to respond but was interrupted, "Just go, goddamn it! Both of you. Go now!" And Cecil turned in his chair to finish his dinner.

4

Later that evening—or more correctly—earlier that morning after Eddie McMullen had been put to bed, the four of them, Cecil and Ella Mae Maddy, Dorothy Newland and Nick Valentine sat together in the living room talking—speculating, actually—about what Eddie might have done. None of them went to bed that night.

Then, just before 6:00 a.m., Cecil left for work. Ada's bar opened at six and he'd have to be there. Dorothy Newland and Nick Valentine rode into town with him. Eddie McMullen was up by eight, feeling somewhat better, and Ella Mae fixed him some breakfast, looked him over thoroughly and tried her best to make him presentable.

Eddie McMullen winced in pain while Ella Mae tended to his finger. She snorted unsympathetically, "Hah! This'd really hurt if you were sober. You're still drunk enough you oughtna' feel a damn thing."

"It really hurts," he moaned. "It's been throbbing for hours now."

"You want me to find a doctor? Or take you to the hospital?"

"No, neither one, but thanks," he said in a more moderate tone. "I can't. I'll just have to put up with it. It oughta be better in a day or two."

"You can't get medical help?" asked Ella Mae. "Why not? Did you do something dumb? Or hurt someone?"

"I had to, Mrs. Maddy. The man pulled a gun on me. It was either my life or his."

"Is he dead," choked Ella Mae. "Did you kill someone?"

"I don't really know whether he's dead or not. That's the truth. But I think he probably is; he went down like a sack of cement. I think that's his blood on my jacket; what's on my pants is mine.

"I didn't really mean to get you involved in this mess, Mrs. Maddy, but thanks for everything. I'll see you in a day or so—when I feel a little better."

Later that same day, Ella Mae did as she had been asked and burned Eddie McMullen's blood-stained clothing in their basement fireplace; then, again at her husband's instruction, she drove into the countryside, strewed the ashes from Eddie's clothes along the highway, and threw the pearl-handled revolver into the deepest part of a convenient creek.

Then, on the following day, Wednesday, Cecil Lee read in the local newspaper that a man named Cleveland Chipley had been robbed and shot to death in nearby Troy, Ohio. He mentioned it to his mother, but she told him to forget about it. That same afternoon, Ella Mae showed the news article to her husband. "I know about it," he said. "I saw it in the paper at Ada's. It was my gun, and I may get into some trouble about it, too."

"So," she temporized. "What are you going to do?"

"I been thinkin' about that all day," he said. "It's been a while since I've seen my brother, and I think I oughta' pay him a visit."

"When are you figuring on doing that?" she wanted to know.

"Actually, I thought I'd have you drive me down there this afternoon. You can bring the car back here. Anybody asks, you can tell 'em you think I've gone to Chicago on business. Okay?"

Ella Mae widened her eyes in surprise, "You mean, like now?"

"I mean like right now. This minute. It's no more'n an hour's drive over to Reardon; you can be back here before suppertime."

Ella Mae didn't argue. Ten minutes later they were on their way, and she was indeed back home by six o'clock. Before she left him for the return trip home, Maddy gave her $710 and told her to give it to Eddie. "What's that for?" she asked.

"Never mind," he remarked. "It's just some money I been holdin' for him. It's his money. You just see he gets it."

Unhappily, the next day, when she opened Ada's Bar for him, she found she wasn't able to open the safe. When she telephoned him for assistance, he told her, "Just come get me. I've been thinkin' about it. Ain't no reason for me to run. I didn't do anything wrong."

"I can't come 'till late afternoon," she countered. "There's no one here to cover the Bar till after 4:00. Besides, I haven't seen Eddie yet to give him the..."

"Okay, I got it," he said. "Later today will be fine. Just be sure you see Eddie first. I'll see you when you get here."

And, as instructed, Ella Mae gave Eddie the money that same afternoon, watched him count it, and as soon as she could extricate herself, set out for Reardon. She and Cecil were back in Greenfield shortly after dark.

5

Troy Police Chief John Hennessey and Patrolmen Cheadle and Cruea had arrived at the Chipley residence within a half-hour after the shooting and they had continued their interviews and their search for evidence until the very early hours of December 28, Wednesday morning. They had found the two unfired .32 caliber shells in the area where Chipley's body had lain, and they also learned from the coroner that the murderer had missed several thousand dollars of additional cash in Chipley's pocket. Finally, they were informed that two of the assailant's bullets had passed through the victim's heart, either one of which would have been fatal.

Unhappily, however, they found no hairs, fibers, prints or other physical or forensic evidence of any kind—other than the two spent bullets found by the coroner. Because it had rained most of the night, they were unable to distinguish any footprints or tire tracks. And beyond the recitation of events provided by family members, they learned nothing more from their countless interrogations of the neighbors or other persons deemed likely to have noticed anything or anyone out of the ordinary. Despite the freely proffered help from nearby police departments and the state highway patrol, nothing new or even remotely helpful was discovered.

Then, in early May, Troy City Solicitor William Harrelson received a telephone call from Chief Hennessey. "'Morning, Bill,'" he greeted in his distinctive, relaxed baritone. "I called to wish you a happy birthday, but I'm not gonna sing it, and I didn't get you a present either. What is it? Thirty-five?"

"Thirty-four," Harrelson corrected. "Don't rush me." And, at that relatively young age, he had already achieved a local prominence, first as a perennial tennis champion, and then as one of the county's bright young lawyers. He had partnered with one of the older, more distinguished lawyers some four years earlier to create a two-man law firm that was well respected in the community. "But you didn't call me just to wish me happy birthday. What's up?"

"You're right, but happy birthday anyway. I called to tell you that we just might have a little something on the Chipley murder case."

"Hey, Chief. Even 'a little something' sounds encouraging. Tell me about it." prodded Harrelson.

"Well," came the response. "It may or may not be a whole hell of a lot, but you remember I sent those two bullets—the ones the coroner found in Chipley's clothes—to the BCI at London..."

"Yeah, I remember," said Harrelson. "And they couldn't match them with anything they had. Right?"

"Right," echoed Hennessey. "No real surprise there, 'cause they weren't likely to have the guy's gun in their possession that soon after the killing. It ain't like he'd just up and send it to 'em for comparison."

"You're not about to tell me they've got a match, are you?" asked Harrelson.

"They just might have," said Hennessey. "Remember the burglary job those three punks pulled at Braun Brothers Packing Company?"

"Uh-huh, I remember. It was six or seven weeks after Chipley."

"That's right. It was February 20, to be precise," said Hennessey. "You probably also remember that we caught the perpetrators in short order; we called them the three stooges, guys named Williams, Gardner and Bryarly. A real brain trust."

Harrelson was impressed. "Yeah, I remember the three stooges, but I sure couldn't have said their names."

Hennessey chuckled, "Yeah you could—especially if you were looking at the report I've got in front of me. You probably don't remember that when we got our hands on the three stooges, we also got hold of their four handguns—and sent them over to the BCI also."

"And they got a match?" asked Harrelson, concealing his excitement.

"Well," Hennessey drew it out, "they claim they do. Their report says that one of the Chipley bullets was fired from one of the guns we got from the stooges—a .38-caliber Colt official police revolver. What bothers me is the fact that they couldn't get a match on the second bullet."

W.M. Harrelson

"I still like it," enthused Harrelson. "One match is better than none."

"Well, it's certainly encouraging," said Hennessey. "But I have to wonder about the lack of a match on the second bullet. I'm gonna send both the bullets and the BCI report to the police laboratory in Columbus and see what they think."

"Sounds good to me. I'll call Jim DeWeese—and then we can all wait to see what we hear from Columbus. Do we know which of the stooges had the gun?"

"Actually, we do," said the Chief. "One of them—I don't remember which, but I've got it logged—admitted it was his. Said he got it a coupla years ago from some guy whose name he didn't know and now he claims he's had it in his possession ever since."

"Why would he do that?" asked Harrelson incredulously. "Why admit he'd had a murder weapon in his possession at the time Chipley was killed?" queried Harrelson.

"How'd I know? Go figure," came the terse reply.

Later that same month they caught a real break. It came in the form of a telephone call from the chief of police at Greenfield, Ohio, who advised Chief Hennessey that he had information about the Chipley murder that he found to be credible. Hennessey lost no time in proceeding to Greenfield, accompanied by Harrelson, where the two of them met with the Greenfield police chief, the Greenfield mayor and with Ella Mae Maddy. Ella Mae, who was then separated from her husband, Cecil Maddy, freely volunteered all that she knew of the happenings in Greenfield the night of December 27, 1954, including that which had been related to her by her son and by her husband. On the basis of what she'd seen, heard and suspected, she told both Chief Hennessey and Solicitor Harrelson that she believed that Eddie McMullen had robbed, shot and killed Mr. Chipley with her husband's snub-nosed, pearl-handled revolver—it was "his life or mine," McMullen had said—and that the two men had divided the stolen money between them. She also told them that she had, at her husband's request, burned Eddie's bloodstained clothes and thrown her husband's revolver into a nearby creek. Then, several days later, she said, her husband had forced her to show him just exactly where she had thrown his gun into the creek; she said she had done that, but had adamantly refused to help him look for it. And, she said, as far as she knew, he hadn't found it.

Then, after learning from the Greenfield authorities that both McMullen and Maddy had recently been arrested by Union County authorities on a safe-cracking charge and that McMullen had been temporarily consigned to Lima State Hospital for psychiatric evaluation, Hennessey and Harrelson made a trip to Lima, on June 24, to interview Eddie McMullen. On June 28, precisely half a year from the date of Chipley's murder, an affidavit charging Edward Allen McMullen and Cecil Gordon Maddy with first degree murder was prepared by Solicitor Harrelson, signed by Chief Hennessey and filed with the Troy Mayor's Court, along with proper arrest warrants.

Directly thereafter, the two men were arrested—they were not hard to find since both were already in custody—and, on July 1, both appeared in Paul Kerr's Mayor's Court where they separately entered "Not Guilty" pleas and were remanded to the Miami County Jail to await grand jury action. Both men were ultimately indicted by the September Grand Jury which, in the oft-times arcane language of the law, charged that on or about the twenty-seventh day of December, 1954, the two men:

> *...did willfully, purposely, and of deliberate and premeditated malice kill and murder one Cleveland Chipley, then and there being, by then and there shooting the said Cleveland Chipley, in and upon the heart and twice in the stomach of the said Cleveland Chipley, with a certain revolver, in the said City of Troy, County of Miami and State of Ohio.*

And, on October 15, the two men appeared in the Miami County Court of Common Pleas, with counsel—Marie C. Schmuecker for Maddy and court-appointed Ellis W. Kerr and William M. Dixon for McMullen—and re-entered their respective "Not Guilty" pleas. County Prosecuting Attorney James H. DeWeese, an able, hard-nosed prosecutor, appeared for the State of Ohio and subsequently moved the Court for an order permitting the two men to be tried jointly. The motion was denied and it was determined that they be tried separately, McMullen first, then Maddy.

6

Eddie McMullen's trial was initially scheduled to begin on November 28, but due to the unexplained disappearance of Glen Purdin, whom the Prosecution had subpoenaed as a witness for the State, the trial date was continued, Purdin was located by the FBI and arrested as a material witness, placed under a bond to assure his appearance at trial, and the case was reassigned for trial on January 23 of the new year, 1956.

During his protracted stay at the Miami County Jail awaiting trial, Eddie McMullen was frequently visited by his court-appointed counsel, the Messrs. Kerr and Dixon, for purposes of trial preparation. During those frequent interviews, Eddie consistently and vehemently proclaimed his innocence. "There is no way I could have been a part of this Chipley thing," he stoutly insisted. "I haven't been anywhere close to Troy, Ohio in years. What's more," he continued, "I have an ironclad *alibi*. I can prove beyond any doubt that I was elsewhere that particular night. I have witnesses."

The law of Ohio is such that a defendant in a criminal case who intends to claim *alibi* at trial must give timely notice of such intention to the Prosecution—and that, having done so, he bears the burden of proof concerning the same. "And, more importantly," explained Bill Dixon, "In order to sustain that burden, it will be necessary for you to testify as to where you were at the time in question."

Ellis W. Kerr

"I understand that," Eddie assured. "I want to do that. I want the jury to know I couldn't possibly have done this thing."

Bill Dixon was an excellent young lawyer, approximately the same age as Bill Harrelson. He persisted, "you do fully understand that if you do, in fact, take the witness stand for any purpose—including *alibi*—you will have entirely waived your constitutional right against self-incrimination?"

"I most certainly do," Eddie was adamant. "And I want to do just that. I didn't do this thing and I want everybody to know it."

"And you also understand that if you do take the stand, you will be thoroughly and intensely cross-examined by Mr. DeWeese? Not only as to your *alibi*, but as to every aspect of your defense, including your own personal history?"

"I understand," Eddie professed for the umpteenth time.

"And you need to know that Mr. DeWeese is a tough advocate and a keen cross-examiner," added Dixon, by way of stern admonition.

Eddie McMullen was not to be swayed. "Look," he protested, "You guys need to understand, once and for all, I didn't kill Mr. Chipley—or anybody else—that night, or ever. And I can prove it. Hell, you can tell 'em I'll take a lie detector test. That oughta do it."

Ellis Kerr had listened intently to the colloquy between his co-counsel and their client. He was the older and more experienced of the two; he was, in fact, himself a former prosecutor. He had joined in Dixon's repeated admonitions regarding the pitfalls surrounding the *alibi* defense.

Now, having heard Eddie's offer to submit to a lie detector examination, he couldn't remain silent any longer. "You need to think that one over very carefully," he warned. "That one cuts both ways. The only circumstance under which the State will agree to a lie detector test is if you agree that the results can be admissible in evidence.

Bill Dixon

Now, I know Jim DeWeese will agree to that condition. Are you prepared to do the same?"

"Absolutely," came the confident response. "Set it up. Soon as you can."

Then, on November 23, Kerr and Dixon filed their notice of *alibi* with the Court, and subsequently, on January 18, just before trial, a stipulation was entered into providing that:

> *...the said Edward A. McMullen shall submit to a lie-detector examination, to be given by John E. Reid of Chicago, Illinois, on January 18, 1956, in Troy, Ohio, for the purpose of determining whether or not the said Edward A. McMullen shot and killed one Cleveland Chipley during a robbery on December 27, 1954, for which offense Edward A. McMullen is presently under indictment.*
>
> *It is further agreed and stipulated that the results of the lie-detector examination, in the form of an opinion by the examiner, John E. Reid, may be offered in evidence on behalf of the defendant or on behalf of the prosecution.*

The stipulation was signed by Defendant Edward A. McMullen and by all counsel and was filed with the Court on January 20.

7

Bill Harrelson had advised Jim DeWeese of the report Chief Hennessey had received from the Bureau of Criminal Investigation and that the two .38 caliber slugs, together with the BCI Report, had been sent to the Police Laboratory in Columbus for a second—and confirming—opinion. He had also requisitioned, and received, the .38 police special from the BCI.

"We'll wait," was DeWeese's only comment.

Several weeks later, when Harrelson had called to advise that the Police Laboratory had issued an opinion that both bullets had been fired from the stooge's gun, DeWeese bridled. "Goddamn it," he exploded. "I think they're dead wrong. All our evidence—and it's irrefutable—proves beyond a shadow of a doubt that Eddie McMullen killed Cleveland Chipley with Cecil Maddy's snub-nosed, pearl-handled revolver.

"And," he continued, "the gun the ballistic guys are telling us killed Chipley doesn't have pearl handles and it certainly isn't a snub-nose; it's a police special with a four-inch barrel. What's more, if that Braun Brothers stooge actually had it for two years, like he claims, it sure as hell wasn't used by McMullen to kill Chipley last December.

"Let me have the damn thing—and the bullets. I've got a coupla' guys in Cincinnati I want to look at it. I'm simply not willing to accept that gun as the murder weapon—unless, of course, we can put it into Eddie McMullen's hands."

"I don't think we're gonna be able to do that," Harrelson remarked dourly.

"Neither do I," agreed DeWeese. "I'll send the whole kit and kaboodle to my guys in Cincinnati. Meanwhile, let's both keep quiet about it. I don't see any reason to muddy the waters unnecessarily."

Weeks later, while in DeWeese's office discussing the case, Harrelson inquired as to whether DeWeese had any further word concerning the ballistics reports.

"Actually, I do," he replied. "I sent one micro-photograph to the Dayton Laboratory and another one to the lab in Cincinnati. Both of them called me back and said that their examinations showed that neither of the two bullets came from the stooge's gun. It's a non-issue."

J.H. Deweese

"That's a relief," said Harrelson. "Sounds like we had a potential red herring. That initial BCI report could really have compromised the evidence and produced a great deal of confusion in your case. Will your experts testify at trial?"

"No, they won't," DeWeese responded. "They've refused to get involved in an argument with the BCI; they said they use them too, from time to time, and they don't want to get on the wrong side of them. And," he appended, "keep in mind that ballistics evidence is still controversial. It hasn't yet been proven to be conclusive; our conflicting reports demonstrate their essential unreliability very dramatically."

"So, what are you going to do?" asked Harrelson.

"Wrong question, Bill," said DeWeese. "It's what are *we* going to do. I've asked Judge Porter to appoint you as a Special Assistant Prosecutor to help me try this case. He's agreed to do so forthwith. You've been working with me thus far; you might as well get paid for your time."

Bill Harrelson was a bit taken aback at the news. "Well, thanks," he said. "I'd like to take a more active role, both in the preparation and in the trial itself. I've never been involved in a murder trial before. I'm not sure I'm up to it, but it'll certainly be good experience for me."

"Don't worry about it." Jim DeWeese assured him. "I'll still be lead counsel; you'll sit second chair. But I'll be glad for whatever help you can give me."

"That works for me," replied Harrelson. "But, back to the original question. What are we going to do about the ballistics snafu?"

"*We* are not going to do a damn thing about it," DeWeese responded glibly. "We have an airtight case against Eddie McMullen. We don't have the murder weapon. Ella Mae has told us she threw it into the creek and that Cecil Maddy tried to retrieve it later. We don't know whether he ever found it. The county sheriff had a whole crew of deputies down there dragging the creek for three days and they came up empty. So, we don't have a gun—any gun. And that's exactly what we'll tell the jury. We'll show them a .38 caliber Colt revolver and simply tell them that we make no claim that it's the murder weapon. A prototype will enable them to better understand the evidence—and serve no further purpose."

Bill Harrelson almost stammered. "But what about this other gun? And the BCI ballistics test results?"

"Won't be a factor," came the answer smugly. "It certainly won't be a part of our case and we won't introduce it. The only possible result of submitting contradictory ballistics reports to the jury would be to confuse both the issue and the jury."

Harrelson wasn't satisfied. "And if the defense introduces it?"

"The defense doesn't even know about it," DeWeese answered dryly.

"Don't we have an obligation to tell them about the issue?" asked Harrelson.

"What? And shoot ourselves in the foot?" came the answer that would brook no argument. "I don't think we're under any obligation to help the Defendant confuse the issue with the claim that some other two-bit jerkwater just may have killed Chipley with a gun that nobody can trace to McMullen, then somehow convinced McMullen to flash a wad of cash, ask Glen Purdin to return Cecil Maddy's gun, confess to the murder, ask Ella Mae to burn his bloody clothes, and then plant Chipley's wallet on Maddy's bathroom floor."

Jim DeWeese stopped in mid-tirade just long enough to draw a second breath, then continued in a more moderate fashion. "Look," he argued, "if we had in our possession any manner of remotely credible evidence that would tend to exculpate the Defendant, simple fairness would mandate our turning the same over to his counsel. But that's not what we have here. All we have here is two sets of inconsistent, controversial opinions that cannot conceivably be reconciled with anything we know and can demonstrate beyond a reasonable doubt. Our primary objective is to assure that even-handed justice is done. I see no reason to help the defense confuse and contort the evidence."

"I hear you," said Harrelson, "loud and clear."

"I didn't mean to be loud or to seem domineering about it," smiled DeWeese. "But I do feel strongly about it. And if, God forbid, I'm wrong, I'll take the heat. Meanwhile I'll return the gun and the lab reports to John Hennessey with an instruction to keep them—safely—in his possession."

8

TRIAL IN THE MATTER of the *State of Ohio vs. Edward A. McMullen, Case No. 7624,* began on Monday, January 23, 1956, with Judge David S. Porter presiding. As anticipated, the State was represented by County Prosecuting Attorney, James H. DeWeese and Special Assistant

Prosecuting Attorney, William M. Harrelson; Defendant Edward A. McMullen was represented by attorneys Ellis W. Kerr and William M. Dixon. The Defendant's 17-year-old wife, Carolyn, and his mother, Eva McMullen, were permitted to sit inside the railing that separated the trial participants from the gallery of spectators.

The first two days of trial were consumed with the process of jury selection—that which lawyers refer to as *voir dire*—during which the Court and the lawyers question the prospective jurors from a panel of citizens whose names were previously selected by lot from a jury wheel and summoned to appear for jury duty. Contrary to that which is routinely asserted by most trial lawyers, and is incorrectly confirmed by most dictionaries, the term *voir dire* actually comes to us from the French *voir* (to see) and *dire* (to speak); it provides an opportunity for the lawyers for each side of a controversy to view and to question each prospective juror to determine his or her fitness to hear the evidence and to render a fair and impartial verdict, i.e. a verdict favorable to their clients.

By late Tuesday afternoon, the process was completed and a jury of twelve, with two alternates, was selected, seated in the jury box and sworn to "...well and truly try and a true deliverance make of the issues between the State of Ohio and the Defendant, Edward A. McMullen."

By agreement of the Court and all counsel, the Wednesday morning session consisted of opening statements by counsel for the respective parties. Jim DeWeese, on behalf of the prosecution, first told the jury that he expected the evidence to show, "...beyond a reasonable doubt that Defendant McMullen, on December 27, 1954, at 9:15 p.m. at 115 Madison Avenue in Troy, purposefully, while in premeditation of a robbery, killed Cleveland Chipley."

Bill Dixon responded on behalf of the Defendant that the evidence would

Judge D.S. Porter

show "...beyond any question that McMullen was not in the vicinity of Troy at any time on the day in question and was, in fact, 100 miles or more away at the time of the murder."

The moment the two lawyers had completed their respective opening statements, DeWeese was on his feet to request that the Court permit the jury to visit "...the premises where the alleged murder took place." And, because such a request was essentially standard practice to which there was no objection, arrangements were quickly concluded whereby the Sheriff was to conduct the jury to the crime scene and point out to them specific buildings, alleyways and landmarks as suggested by the lawyers. Any questions on the part of the jurors were to be addressed only to the Sheriff, who would, in turn, refer them to Judge Porter for response within the rigid framework of the law. There was, of course, to be no conversation concerning the case between the jurors and any of the lawyers—or with the Defendant, Eddie McMullen, who had elected to attend the "jury view." The purpose of the exercise, Judge Porter admonished the jury "was not to gather evidence, but only to enable you to better understand the evidence as it comes to you from the testimony of the witnesses and from those exhibits which may be admitted into evidence during the trial."

Because the scene of the "alleged" crime was no more than ten blocks from the courthouse, the view itself consumed less than an hour's time and after a short recess, the jurors were back in the box by 11:00 a.m.

Court was again in session and Judge Porter nodded to Jim DeWeese and invited, "Mr. Prosecutor, you may call your first witness."

That first witness turned out to be Glen G. McConnell, Jr., who was actually examined by Special Assistant Prosecutor Bill Harrelson. McConnell testified that he was a graduate of Ohio State University, with degrees in both architecture and civil engineering, and was currently employed as City of Troy Engineer. Harrelson handed him State's Exhibit 1 and asked him to identify it.

"That is a drawing which I made from field notes of part of Inlot 598 in the City of Troy and the buildings thereon," McConnell answered confidently.

Further questioning elicited that the residence address of the property was 115 North Madison, that the sketch was drawn to a scale of five feet to the inch and that the witness had prepared it the preceding day. After a few more questions from both Harrelson and Kerr, the Exhibit was admitted into evidence by agreement of the parties. McConnell's testimony, both direct and on cross-examination, had taken less than five minutes.

Robert Leffel, Sr., Cleve Chipley's brother-in-law, was the State's second witness. He was also examined by Bill Harrelson on direct and was subsequently cross-examined by Ellis Kerr. His testimony concerning the events of the evening of December 27, 1954, was entirely consistent with the reports he had previously made to Chief Hennessey and to Police Officers Cheadle and Cruea—and thereafter reiterated from time to time—as the case had wended its way through the judicial process. This time, he was aided by the drawing prepared by the City Engineer, which enabled him to point out to the jury the various locations to which he referred, i.e. where he was when he heard the three shots fired, the route he had taken when he returned to the house, the relationship of the buildings, light-posts and other landmarks, one to the other, and where it was he had found the victim.

Ellis Kerr's cross-examination of Mr. Leffel was brief and essentially caused the witness to confirm his prior testimony. He was successful in securing an acknowledgment that Mr. Leffel hadn't gotten a good look at Chipley's assailant and could neither describe the man nor the path of his departure, but that acknowledgment was also entirely consistent with his prior statements.

The elder Mr. Leffel was followed to the witness stand by his son, William Leffel, who was examined by Jim DeWeese. William, or "Bill" Leffel testified that he had been in the U. S. Army for two and a half years and was at that time stationed at Fort Belvoir, Virginia. He had been home for the Christmas holidays in late December of 1954, and, on the twenty-seventh of that month he had been at his uncle's home at 115 North Madison Avenue in Troy. Those present that evening were his uncle, Cleveland Chipley, his aunt Della, his parents, and his wife, Patricia. He wasn't asked, and therefore didn't mention, that he and Patricia had just returned from a short honeymoon. Then, at Jim DeWeese's prompting, he told the jury all that he had seen, heard, observed and done that rainy evening. Like his father before him, his testimony was entirely consistent with his prior statements to the investigating police officers.

Bill Leffel told the jury that the back doorbell had rung and his aunt had answered it, then come back into the room and said something to his uncle;

that his uncle had then got up from where he had been sitting and went to the back door. Shortly thereafter, he said, his aunt re-entered the room and asked him and his father to follow her husband out to his shop.

"We put our coats on and proceeded to walk down to the used furniture shop," he said. "We got about halfway down to the shop, when all of a sudden he was hollering and screaming for help."

"Who was?" demanded DeWeese.

"My uncle, Mr. Chipley. He hollered 'Dell, Dell!' a few times and then he started hollering 'Help!' We just started to move a little faster and then there were three shots fired, all fired consecutively, no hesitation between each one."

"Tell the jury what you did next," prompted DeWeese.

"I turned and started back to the house. As I got back to the house and got underneath the porch light, I looked back to the shop. The outside light was turned off and a man stepped out and looked toward the house—maybe a second or two—then turned and walked down the alley."

Later on in the colloquy between the Prosecutor and the witness, there came the question, "Can you give the jury some description of the man you saw that night?"

"I think so," came the answer. "He was wearing tan clothing, like army-type khaki, and something like a windbreaker, also tan. The shirt I couldn't really tell about. His hair was sort of a sandy color and it looked as though it was a little bit messed up."

"Anything about his size or height?"

"He was fairly tall, I imagine about six feet tall and kind of thin—as best I could tell."

The young soldier told of his own activities immediately after the shooting, how he'd gotten into his truck and driven around the neighborhood, seen the ambulance with his father at Zwiebel's corner, returned to the house and made statements to the investigating officers.

Before DeWeese released him for cross-examination, he took care to ask whether he had, since that night, "...seen anyone who resembled the person you saw standing outside the door that evening."

Leffel's affirmative response to the question caused the jury to perk up their collective ears, during the first part of November, just two months before the trial, he said, "I was taken to a line-up at the Miami County jail in which nine or ten men were present. At that time I picked out one man that resembled the man I had seen that evening."

"Were you told who it was?" asked DeWeese.

"I was told at that time it was McMullen."

Ellis Kerr's cross-examination of Bill Leffel, while valiant in its nature and extent, actually accomplished little more than confirm his testimony on direct. Kerr attempted to test the witness's description of the man he'd seen outside his uncle's shop after the shots were fired. Hadn't he previously described him as slightly shorter than six feet tall? Wasn't the alleyway poorly lighted that evening? Was the outside light burning? Did he really get a good look at the man? Wasn't it pretty dark that night? And, of course it was raining too, wasn't it? The visibility was less than ideal? How certain was he that the man he'd picked from the police line-up was the man he'd seen outside his uncle's shop nearly two years before?

Despite his skill as an advocate, and his yeoman-like efforts to shake Leffel's testimony, Ellis Kerr ultimately failed to neutralize its effect. The witness's candid acknowledgment that he could have been mistaken, but didn't believe that he was, actually made his account of the events and his description of the perpetrator more credible.

Because both of the examiners announced to the Court that they were finished with their questions, the young soldier was released. And, because it was lunchtime, Judge Porter declared a recess until 1:15.

The testimony rendered by the first two witnesses called during the Wednesday afternoon session was essentially perfunctory. Police Officers Virgil Cruea and Jack Cheadle related to the jury the details of their activities and their investigations on the night of December 27, 1954, from the time they first received the call to the Chipley residence until they had completed and filed their official reports. Chief of Police John Hennessey repeated and confirmed the testimony of his officers and added a description of his own activities, both on the night of the shooting and subsequent to that event.

Prosecutor Jim DeWeese also questioned Chief Hennessey about the .32 caliber revolver and matching shells discovered near the spot where Chipley had been found. Hennessey described the weapon and characterized it as being "in poor mechanical shape" in that the bullets would fall out of the chamber when the gun was held in an upright position. DeWeese then handed Hennessey the revolver, marked as State's Exhibit 2 and asked him to demonstrate that fact to the jury. In response to DeWeese's request, the witness loaded the live shells into the revolver and inclined it upwards. Three of the newly inserted bullets fell out of the gun and onto the carpeted courtroom floor.

"I take it," mused DeWeese wryly, "that a gun in good working condition is not supposed to operate that way?"

"No, sir," answered Hennessey. "Most guns will have a guard over here where this gun is open," he pointed to the rear of the revolver chamber and added, "...a modern gun will."

Asked what else his officers had found, Chief Hennessey responded, "I found on one of the bullets that was still in the chamber an indication that made it appear that it had been struck by the hammer of the gun in attempting to fire the gun."

"Had the bullet, which has now been marked as State's Exhibit 3, been discharged?"

"No, sir, it had not."

DeWeese then handed the witness State's Exhibit 4, a composite of four live shells, and asked him to tell the jury what it was.

"Two of these shells are the ones found in the cylinder of the .32 revolver, and the other two are the ones that were picked up off the floor of Mr. Chipley's shop."

DeWeese then offered Exhibits 2, 3 and 4 into evidence, and they were admitted without objection. And, at DeWeese's request, they were passed around to the individual jurors for their inspection.

Exhibits 5 and 6 were shown to Hennessey with a request for identification. He answered without hesitation, "These are slugs that have been fired from a .38 caliber shell."

"How did you happen to have possession of them?"

"I was at the funeral home when Mr. Chipley's body was undressed and these were recovered from his clothing."

"Mr. Hennessey, just so there will be no misunderstanding about these slugs that you have identified as being .38's, would you tell the jury whether these are slugs that could be related to the gun we have in evidence as a .32 caliber—is there any relationship between the slugs and the .32 caliber gun?"

"No, sir, there is not.

"Would it be possible to fire these .38 caliber slugs from the .32 caliber gun?"

"It would be impossible," came the answer.

Finally, before he let the witness go, DeWeese reminded him that it was he who had signed and filed the initial affidavit charging the Defendant and causing his arrest. Upon that predicate, he asked, "Can you tell us the circumstances leading up to the filing of that affidavit?"

Hennessey had been in court before, and therefore possessed more than a rudimentary understanding of the so-called "hearsay rule" which would have prevented him from repeating matters which had been related to him by persons outside the presence of the Defendant. In that context, his response to the question was truly artful. "On May 17, 1955, I received a call from the Chief of Police of Greenfield, Ohio, stating that he had some information in the Chipley murder. City Solicitor William Harrelson and I went to Greenfield that night, arriving there about 8:30 p.m. We contacted the Chief of Police, the Mayor of Greenfield and a Mrs. Cecil Maddy, and received some information from them. On the basis of that information an affidavit and warrant was filed against Edward McMullen on the twenty-eighth of June."

Ellis Kerr's cross-examination of Chief Hennessey was, as might have been expected, both skillful and thorough—but nonetheless brief and unproductive. He did ask whether he had caused any ballistic tests made on the two slugs found in Mr. Chipley's clothing. In response, Hennessey answered truthfully, "I took them to the State Bureau of Investigation at London, Ohio, on January 6, 1955 to ascertain what kind of gun they were fired from. Mr. Fred Dingler examined these bullets and said they were definitely fired from a .38 Colt revolver."

"Did the ballistic test show they were fired from the same gun?" asked Kerr.

The answer was a simple and uninformative, "They didn't test them for that."

Kerr also inquired about a report the Department had received from a local service station operator the day after Chipley was shot and killed.

"We have a report of that, yes, sir."

Kerr then handed the Chief a copy of the written police report, now marked as Defendant's Exhibit A, and asked him to read it.

Hennessey confirmed that the exhibit was a true copy of his own official report and read it to the jury. "7:05 p.m. December 28 contacted by Ralph Moyer of Moyer's Service Station and he reported about 7 p.m. last night a subject entered the station and asked about a secondhand furniture store. He couldn't remember the name and when Ralph named Chipley's this subject stated that this was the man he was looking for. He didn't know the town and Moyer directed him to the Chipley residence. Moyer described this subject as 25, about 5'7", 140 to 145 pounds, thin face, straight dirty blond hair combed back, wearing dark gray work trousers and a short grayish jacket. Ralph stated he could identify this man if seen because he paid particular attention to him. He thought it odd that a young man like that would be buying used furniture. He didn't notice any car at all."

Then, by way of follow-up, Kerr inquired, "Since the time that you brought Mr. McMullen back to Troy on June 30, 1955, did you ever take Mr. Moyer to confront him for the purpose of identification?"

"No, I did not. I took a picture of Mr. McMullen to Mr. Moyer's service station for that purpose; he said he wasn't sure. He said the picture resembled the man he'd seen, but he couldn't be positive."

With that response, the witness was excused, and because it was not yet three o'clock, the Prosecution was able to work through two additional "short witnesses." Miami County Coroner William Adkins described the wounds which he had found on the body of Cleve Chipley and told of his having found two slugs in his clothing. Although he testified that the deceased had suffered three separate wounds, he could find only two exit wounds and therefore concluded that a third slug remained in his body. The immediate cause of death, he stated, was the single slug that penetrated both chambers of his heart. There was no cross-examination and Dr. Adkins was excused.

Cleveland Chipley's son, Melvin Chipley, was the final witness Wednesday afternoon. He testified that he received a call at about 9:15 the evening of December 27, and because he resided within a block of his father's shop, he arrived on the scene within minutes. He had knelt by his father and taken both his hands in his own and looked into his eyes. He noted a large roll of bills in his left pants and heard his mother remark, "At least, they didn't get his money." As she stood there wringing her hands, she added, "His pocketbook, his pocketbook." Then he checked his inside jacket pocket and discovered that his pocketbook was, indeed, missing.

Bill Harrelson, who had conducted Melvin's examination, asked how his father's death had affected his mother's health and what her condition had been since her husband's death.

"Very emotional," he answered. "She had suffered a light stroke soon after Dad died and, about two weeks ago, she had a heart attack."

Ellis Kerr asked Melvin several pointed questions about the large sums of money Cleve Chipley was reputed to carry about his person, the witness was excused, and Court was adjourned for the day.

Later that afternoon, Jim DeWeese and Bill Harrelson were seated across the desk from one another in the Prosecutor's office, located on the third floor of the courthouse building, just across the atrium from the courtroom in which they had spent the better part of the last three days. It had become their custom to sit down together, at the conclusion of each day's court session, to reprise that day's testimony, speculate as to the jurors' reaction to the proceedings and the evidence presented, and most importantly, to refine their agenda for the presentation of the next day's evidence. The Prosecutor's office was not equipped with a wet-bar, but DeWeese did keep a bottle and a glass or two in his right-hand drawer for purposes of post-trial relaxation.

It was nearly 7:00 in the evening when their assessment and planning session had wound to a conclusion and each of them had finished their drinks. Bill Harrelson, in re-visiting the testimony of Chief Hennessey, couldn't resist a final comment, "I will say to you, Jim, that I was a little surprised that Ellis Kerr didn't ask John whether or not the crime lab had developed any further information concerning the two slugs, or if they'd ever come into possession of a weapon that matched their markings. I had really kind of expected him to press that point."

"Actually, Bill, there was nothing in the Chief's testimony to suggest that further probing would have been fruitful. I'm not really surprised he didn't go there; I hadn't expected him to. All the same, I'm just as glad the question didn't come up. I don't want to see an issue created where none should exist. "And," he mused, "we both know that those two guys won't miss any opportunity to confuse the jury. It's about the only chance they have to win an acquittal."

9

Trial in the matter of State v. McMullen resumed Thursday morning in the most innocuous manner imaginable. The prosecution first called Cleve Chipley's daughter, Mary Tooley, to the witness stand for examination by Bill Harrelson concerning her own personal knowledge of her father's custom of keeping large sums of money on his person. She said that she resided at 115 ½ North Madison Avenue, in an apartment above her parents' residence. It had been her wont to help her father manage his used furniture store from time to time, and, in that context, had access to his roll of bills and the contents of his wallet. She described the wallet itself, together with the contents of the same which she had often noted, including her father's fishing license, driver's license, social security card, and most significantly, the several large denominations of bills he carried in a zippered compartment in the old, soft leather pocketbook she had described.

In fact, she told the jury, she had helped her father in the store the afternoon of the day of his murder. Between 5:00 and 5:30, a young couple had stopped to buy a nightstand and her father had handed her his pocketbook and asked her to make change.

The next witness, Eldon Newland, was interrogated by Jim DeWeese. He testified that he was a resident of Greenfield, Ohio, and had been a policeman in Greenfield for the past three years. DeWeese handed Newland an item, which had been marked State's Exhibit 7 and asked whether he could identify it.

"That is a .38 Special Colt, commonly known as a snub-nose revolver," he answered as if on cue. "I used to own one very similar to this, but that one had genuine pearl grips and was heavier than this. It wasn't larger in size, but was made of a different metal which made it heavier."

"Do you still own the gun you've just described?" asked DeWeese.

"No, sir. I sold it at the end of May, 1954."

"To whom did you sell it?" pressed DeWeese.

"I sold it to Cecil Maddy of Greenfield."

Ellis had only one question of Officer Newland, "Is there anything unique or unusual about this weapon?"

"No, sir. It is quite a common gun."

If the morning's bland, but technically necessary testimony had had a soporific effect on the twelve jurors, the next witness quickly provided an antidote. Cecil Lee Maddy was capably induced by Bill Harrelson to relate in infinite detail all that he knew about the events of the evening of December 27 and the early morning hours of the twenty-eighth. He told of Eddie McMullen's late arrival on the twenty-seventh, looking for his father, and his having subsequently heard his father enter the house with another man when he had gotten up to go to learn who was there. He said that he hadn't actually seen either of the two men at that time, but heard his father tell him to go back to bed. He did so and, perhaps half an hour later, he heard the two men leave.

"Then what did you do?" asked Harrelson.

"I got up to see what was going on—and I went to the bathroom."

"What, if anything, did you observe in the bathroom?"

"There was a khaki-like, air force jacket lying on the floor."

"Did you inspect the jacket?"

"Yes, sir. I found an old, dark wallet in the pocket. I looked into it and found a driver's license."

"Whose driver's license was it?" persisted Harrelson.

"Cleveland Chipley."

And, at Harrelson's prompting, Cecil Lee told of finding his father's snub-nosed .38 Special revolver with mother of pearl handles, lying on his father's bed. He had no difficulty in recognizing it as belonging to his father because he'd cleaned it from time to time at his father's request. His father usually kept the gun by his bedside or under the mattress, though he did carry it to work occasionally. He told the jury that he had examined the gun and found that it contained three spent shells.

"What happened then?"

"I went back to bed; then still later—around 2:30—some people came to our home and I got up to investigate. It was my mother and father and another couple, Miss Newland and a man named Valentine—and Eddie McMullen—he was there too. They were all in the kitchen."

Upon further questioning, he told the jury that he had read about a man named Cleveland Chipley being shot in Troy. He said he hadn't told anyone other than his mother about his having found the wallet containing Chipley's driver's license.

Ellis Kerr's cross-examination was both thorough and protracted, but he was unable to shake Cecil Lee's testimony in the slightest degree. The most he was able to accomplish was to establish that the boy had spent three days before Christmas that year in a Columbus jail because he and two of his friends had shot out some windows with a BB gun.

The next witness, Glenn Harold Purdin, immediately commanded the jurors' eager attention. Also examined by Bill Harrelson, he acknowledged that he had left the area after the murder charge had been filed against Eddie McMullen. He had wanted to avoid having to testify. The FBI had picked him up in early November and he was held in the Miami County Jail as a material witness until trial. His appearance at trial was scarcely voluntary.

In response to Harrelson's questioning, Purdin related to the jury the events of December 27 as he remembered them. He told of Eddie McMullen's having come by the Smoke Shop that evening between eleven o'clock and midnight to buy back the check Purdy had been given earlier and to ask him to return the .38 revolver to Cecil Maddy. Purdin said that as soon as he had finished closing up the Smoke Shop, he went to Ada's Bar and delivered the gun to Maddy. Then, perhaps an hour later, he said, McMullen had asked him to drive him to Club 28. He had no recollection of McMullen's clothing or personal appearance that night except for the fact that he had a bandage on his hand.

During the course of his cross-examination by Ellis Kerr, Purdin said that he had fled the jurisdiction because of what he was told by Ella Mae Maddy the following Wednesday, December 29. "She showed me a newspaper account of the Chipley murder and said that's what Eddie had done."

Once again Kerr's cross-examination failed to shake the witness's testimony on direct. He did establish that Purdin and his wife were close friends of the Maddys and that Purdin had never discussed the case with anyone other than Ella Mae; he had most certainly had no discussion with either Cecil Maddy or with Eddie McMullen. He also described the patrons he had seen that night at Ada's and confirmed that the place was very lively that evening with Cecil and Valentine buying drinks for everybody.

Then, after the lunch-break, Bill Harrelson asked again about his having fled to avoid having to testify.

"Well," came the answer, "I was scared."

"What were you scared of?"

"Possibly physical harm to me or my family."

And when Ellis Kerr, on re-direct examination asked Purdin if he had ever received any threats, the answer must have come as a surprise. "Well, not any threats, no, sir. Late last summer, I'd moved to Troy and one time after that I was coming out of the Orchard Tavern just out of town here on a Sunday night and some stranger said to me, 'Your name is Purdin, isn't it?' I said, 'Yes, why?' and he said, 'You're not going to be a witness in that trial, are you?' I said 'I don't know.'"

"When did that occur?" asked Kerr.

"November. Just before I left the state."

Dorothy Newland was the thirteenth witness called by the State. She had a clear memory of the events of the night of December 27, 1954 because, she explained, "It was the first time that I was ever out to Cecil and Ella Mae's house and the first time I was ever out with this Nicholas Valentine. It was the Monday after Christmas."

Her direct examination was conducted by Jim DeWeese and was actually concluded in less than five minutes. She told the jury that she and "Nick Balentino—or Valentine," she wasn't sure which it was—had left Ada's together and arrived at the Maddy residence at 2:30 in the morning of the twenty-eighth. Those persons present at the Maddy home that morning were she and Balentino, Ella Mae and Cecil Maddy. Jim DeWeese asked her directly, "Did you see anyone else there?"

"No, I did not ... yes, I did, I seen Eddie McMullen."

"When did you see him?"

"That was around three o'clock. That would be on the twenty-eighth. I was in the living room and I saw him walk from the kitchen through the living room to the bedroom."

Because of Eddie McMullen's plea of *alibi*—that he was somewhere else that night, DeWeese wanted to nail down the fact of his presence at the Maddy residence. For that reason, he pressed the point. "And you saw him?"

"Yes, I saw him."

"That was about three o'clock on the morning of December 28?"

"That's right."

"Did you know Eddie McMullen?"

"Yes."

"How well did you know him?"

"I went to school with him in the second and third grades."

"And you are positive it was Eddie McMullen who walked through the living room from the kitchen to the bedroom?" persisted DeWeese.

"Yes."

Fully satisfied that he had made his point, DeWeese turned the witness over to Kerr for what proved to be an extensive, probing, yet altogether fruitless cross-examination. Despite his best efforts, he was unable to shake or to undermine her testimony. She had left no doubt that Eddie McMullen had been present that night at the Maddy residence.

10

After a short recess, DeWeese called Ella Mae Maddy as his final witness that day. He skillfully guided her through her own background, the several residences she and her family had occupied in the Greenfield area during 1954 and 1955, the members of her family—her former husband, Cecil, and her two sons—and the fact that one of their residences was located on a farm owned by Cecil's aunt, Ada Whitley, who, just incidentally, was also the owner of Ada's Bar where Cecil was employed as manager.

Ella Mae had a clear recollection of the evening of December 27. She had been at home, fed her two sons their supper, and waited for her husband to come home for his own supper. She waited until "about a quarter of eight" when he telephoned and asked her to come to Ada's bar. She had done so and sat with her husband at the bar until just before closing time. Dorothy Newland and Nick Valentine had sat with them also. At about midnight, she said, Glen Purdin came in the front door and motioned for Cecil to "come up front." He had done so and talked with Purdin awhile. Then he had poured himself a shot of whiskey and went through the back door and into the storage area. A few minutes later he signaled her to join him there. When she appeared there as he had directed, he told her to bring her car around to the back door. Without knowing why he had asked her to do so, she left the bar, got into her Buick automobile, which had been parked on the street in front of the bar and drove it through an adjoining alley to the service entrance to the bar.

"What happened then?" DeWeese wanted to know.

"A door opened and a voice said 'Come in,'" she answered.

"Do you know whose voice that was?"

"Not at the time. Not until I went in."

"Did you go into the building?"

"Yes."

"Who was in there?"

"Eddie McMullen."

"Did you have any conversation with Mr. McMullen at that time?"

"I walked in and he looked at me, he was holding up his left hand, and he said...you want me to say his exact words?"

"Yes," responded DeWeese, "His exact words."

"He said, 'The son-of-a-bitch pulled a rod on me, but I don't think he'll be able to pull it on anyone else.'"

"Tell the jury about his left hand."

"The little finger was all bloody; the nail was broken and the flesh was gone."

Ella Mae told the jury that Cecil and Eddie McMullen next spent some time together in the back room, then at the bar, and finally in a booth. When she came to the booth she noted that McMullen was sick and told her husband to take him to the back room. The two men retired to the storage room and she next saw them some 45 minutes later when they came in the front door of the bar. McMullen had obviously changed his clothes from the air force jacket he'd been wearing to her husband's yellow corduroy shirt. She also noticed that his finger had been bandaged. The two men joined her at the bar and they remained there until "almost closing time" when her husband told her to go home. Acting on that instruction, she, in company with Dorothy Newland and Nick Valentine, drove to her home and settled in the living room. Shortly thereafter, she said, she heard Cecil and Eddie McMullen come into the kitchen. She entered the kitchen, found them sitting at her kitchen table, warmed up and served them the supper she had prepared for Cecil some seven or eight hours earlier, and sat down with them.

Not surprisingly, Ella Mae's testimony was the most damaging evidence offered by the State in its efforts to secure Eddie McMullen's conviction for murder in the first degree. In response to Jim DeWeese's questioning, she told the jury all that had transpired that evening and over the following days. She told them of having earlier overheard Cecil ask McMullen, "How strong did you go?" and McMullen's having failed to answer, but simply dropping his head and remaining silent. She also related that McMullen had been too sick to eat the supper she had prepared and that he had first asked permission, then gone to bed in the Maddys' bedroom. She told the jurors that each of the two men had separately instructed her to burn McMullen's clothing.

"What did you do with those clothes?" asked DeWeese.

"Took them downstairs and burned them in the fireplace."

"Did you observe anything unusual about the clothes?"

"Little spots of blood here and there. Not a whole lot, just small spots."

She also told of her having treated McMullen's finger the following morning; of her husband's flight to Reardon, Ohio, to "visit with his brother," his instruction that she give McMullen a roll of bills totaling $710, and her having done so that same day, and, most significantly, of McMullen's candid admission to her that he had robbed and shot Cleveland Chipley.

"I asked him," she said, "if he had heard the news? And he said, 'That's right, I've read the paper' and I asked him 'Eddie, is this what you did?' and his face shook and he turned white and he said 'Yes, I had to, Mrs. Maddy. It was me or him. He pulled a rod on me and it was my life or his.'"

And, just before he released her, DeWeese prompted her to speak to the jury of her husband's later telling her that it was his gun that had been used in the Chipley affair and that he had asked her to return the $710 to McMullen because it had been given to him on the twenty-seventh to hold for him. "It was Eddie's money, he'd said, and I was just holding it for him."

Jim DeWeese glanced toward the jury box to guess whether Ella Mae's testimony had resonated with them, then looked askance to Bill Harrelson, whose imperceptible nod seemed to assure him, resumed his seat at the counsel table and announced to the Court, "No further questions."

Both Ellis Kerr and Bill Dixon were well aware of the damage that had been wreaked on their client's *alibi* defense by the cumulative testimony of Cecil Lee Maddy, Glen Purdin, Dorothy Newland—and most especially—that of Ella Mae Maddy. Unless they could, in some fashion or other, neutralize the effect of the State's evidence, the likely result of the trial would be a conviction. With that consideration, Ellis Kerr labored long and hard to destroy—or at the very least—to undermine Ella Mae's credibility. His cross-examination consumed the balance of the afternoon and continued on into the Friday morning session.

He challenged virtually every statement she'd made on direct examination, demanding that she be certain as to each date, event or activity she'd described or alluded to, the names and dates of every conversation she'd had with any person, be it a friend, acquaintance or police officer or other enforcement official. He demanded why it was that she had done her husband's bidding with reference to Eddie McMullen, burned his clothes and scattered the ashes along the highway, disposed of the gun, drove her husband into hiding at Reardon, delivered the $710 to Eddie McMullen—and kept quiet about the entire matter until the late spring of 1955.

"Because that's what my husband told me to do," she answered.

"Did you always do what he told you to do?" Kerr persisted.

"Yes, sir," she said. "If I knew what was good for me, I did."

"Explain that answer, please," demanded Kerr.

"Cause if I didn't, I'd get a good beating," she explained.

Kerr took that answer and ran with it. Wasn't it true that Cecil Maddy had beaten her frequently? Wasn't it also true that she and Maddy became estranged in the spring of 1955? And that she had filed for divorce in June of that same year? At about the same time she had reported her husband's involvement in the Chipley murder?

And, although Kerr did not directly articulate it, the suggestion that she'd made her report to the authorities and had now supported it with her testimony out of sheer spite—retribution against her husband for his persistent mistreatment of her over the years—could not have been lost on the jury.

Why else, he seemed to inquire, would she have waited until June of 1955—nearly half a year—to report what she professed to know to the authorities.

"I was afraid of what might happen if I'd reported it. Afraid for myself—and afraid for the boys, our sons. They were both in school and if this had all come out, they'd have been mortified."

"Then why report it at all?" demanded Kerr. You'd waited until June, when you filed your divorce action. Why then, if not..."

"Actually," interrupted Ella Mae, "I did tell Officer Newland about it in either March or April, but I asked him to keep it in confidence until school was out so as not to cause our sons any more humiliation than was necessary. He was good enough to treat it that way."

Then, almost as in desperation, Kerr asked about whether she and Eddie McMullen were seeing one another, whether she'd had affairs with Glen Purdin, Nick Valentine or with Dorothy Newland. He pressed her about what he perceived to be inconsistencies and contradictions in her testimony, but it was all in vain. Ella Mae's testimony held up under fire and her credibility remained intact.

That which he did accomplish—inadvertently—was to cause her to describe her husband's fruitless search of the creek bed in an attempt to re-locate his gun. That description seemed, in and of itself, to corroborate her entire story.

And finally, late Friday morning, he gave it up. "Nothing further," he conceded and sat down heavily in his chair at the counsel table.

The State's final witness came as an unanticipated surprise to the jury. Jim DeWeese called Lie Detector Expert John E. Reid of Chicago to the stand and questioned him first concerning his background, his education, training and experience in the science of bio-mechanical lie detection. It was a process necessary to establish his credentials in the field and to thereby "qualify" him as an expert witness whose opinion as to an esoteric matter—one outside the common experience—could be expressed to the jury and considered as evidence.

John Reid, in response to DeWeese's questioning, explained the underlying principles, the theories, the practical mechanics and the methodology of the lie detector process and equipment, the manner in which it operated to determine by his physical responses whether a person's answers to pre-determined questions were truthful by measuring his blood pressure, his pulse and his respirations as he answered the questions posed to him by the administrator. Most of the questions were essentially irrelevant and innocuous, he said, and a scattered few were pointed and directed to the principal issues under scrutiny.

By way of practical demonstration, and at Jim DeWeese's request, Reid "hooked-up" Bill Harrelson to the various electrical leads and items of physical response-measuring equipment which were a part of the lie detector device that he had used when testing Eddie McMullen at the county jail just days before the trial. Then, in full presence of the jury, he questioned him in the same manner as that which he had utilized with Eddie McMullen. He even challenged Harrelson to deliberately lie to one or more of his questions to see if he could "beat the machine." As it happened, he could not. At the conclusion of the demonstration, Reid passed the recorder's tape among the jurors for their examination, and Harrelson conceded that the tape clearly identified those answers that were untruthful.

Reid told the jury that he had asked McMullen a series of questions about matters concerning which there would be no reason for him to lie, interspersing those clearly innocuous questions, from time to time, with others which were both unanticipated by the Defendant and directly relevant to the circumstances of the Chipley murder. Among the questions put to the Defendant were, "Did you steal the billfold? Did you shoot Chipley? Was the light turned out in Chipley's store? Did the man who killed Chipley ask to buy a stove? Did you tell Mrs. Maddy 'I had to kill him; it was either him or me?'"

Although Reid testified that all of these pointed questions produced a demonstrable reaction, recorded on a recording tape, the most significant, compelling reaction came with the final question.

After guiding Reid through his testimony, Jim DeWeese asked his own final question, "Mr. Reid, based upon your education, training and experience, and upon your administration of the lie detector test to Defendant Edward McMullen, do you have an opinion which you can express to a reasonable degree of scientific certainty, as to whether or not Mr. McMullen answered your questions truthfully?

"Yes, sir," Reid answered. "I have such an opinion."

"What is that opinion?" asked DeWeese in the protocol mandated by the rules of evidence.

"In my opinion, Mr. McMullen was not telling the truth," came the anticipated response. "There were measurable reactions to all of the crucial questions; there would have been no such reactions at all if he had answered truthfully."

Ellis Kerr's cross-examination only confirmed Reid's testimony on direct. He did elicit an acknowledgment that Eddie McMullen had been cooperative and appropriately responsive to all the questions put to him, but he was wholly unable to undermine the testimony in chief.

No sooner had the witness been released, when Jim DeWeese moved the Court to admit all of the State's exhibits into evidence, and when that motion had been granted, he announced, "If it please the Court, the State rests its case."

And, because it was late in the day, Judge Porter reiterated his customary admonitions to the jurors—that they were not to discuss the matter with anyone, or to read newspaper accounts of the trial, or attempt to reach any decisions on their own until all the evidence was in—and released the jury for the weekend. The Defense would present its evidence, he said, beginning Monday morning.

Jim DeWeese and Bill Harrelson packed their briefcases and hustled themselves across the hall to the Prosecutor's inner office. It had been a long and arduous week of trial and they were relieved that the State had concluded its case in chief; it had seemed as though the ball had been in their court the entire time—as, indeed, it had been. The prosecution always bears the burden of proof and dare not fail to prove any single element of the charges against the accused. They clearly were not yet finished with the matter, but, as DeWeese expressed it, "At least the monkey is off our backs." Besides, they had the weekend to regroup, to gather their resources and their wits, before Ellis Kerr and Bill Dixon presented their side of the issue.

Settled then, in their padded seats across DeWeese's desk, glasses in hand, the two men rehashed and re-lived their week in court. Had they missed or omitted anything of importance? Were there questions they should have asked? Objections they should have presented?

And when they had satisfied themselves that their presentation had gone as well as they might have hoped, Bill Harrelson asked the inevitable question. "What do you think, Jim? Do we win this thing? Have we got enough for a conviction?"

Jim DeWeese set his glass down on his desk blotter with careful deliberation; it was his third and his attitude had appropriately mellowed. "Oh yeah," he pronounced confidently. "We'll convict the bastard—and it shouldn't take the jury very long to reach a verdict."

"You seem very certain about it," commented Harrelson. "We haven't heard their evidence yet. I'm a little concerned about this *alibi* claim—and, of course, they have the benefit of the 'beyond a reasonable doubt standard.'"

"I'm not at all concerned," said DeWeese, replacing his flask into his desk drawer with finality. "His *alibi* will be seen for just exactly what it is, a desperate, last-ditch effort on the part of his family and friends to save his neck, even if they have to perjure themselves to do it."

"Besides," he added with a twinkle, "We don't have to convict him. He's already done that himself."

"How's that?" asked Harrelson.

"Think about it," said DeWeese. "If the dummy had simply 'lost' Maddy's gun and Chipley's wallet, gone straight home to bed, burned his bloody clothes, and kept his mouth shut, no one would have ever been the wiser and he'd have gotten away clean.

"But what does our budding genius do?" he asked rhetorically. "He drives direct to Maddy's home to return the gun, then seeks out Purdin, flashes a wad of cash and asks him to return the gun—with three spent shells still in the chamber, no less—to Maddy. The next thing he does is to show up at Ada's, still wearing bloody clothes—plus a badly damaged finger—flashes more cash around, and finally admits to both Maddy and Ella Mae, on more than one occasion, that he'd pulled the robbery and shot Chipley. And, of course, he leaves his bloody clothes in Maddy's bathroom with a wallet containing Chipley's driver's license in it.

"How bright is all that?"

"Not very," conceded Harrelson. "When you put it that way, I guess he has virtually convicted himself out of his own mouth—and his own actions."

"Right on," said DeWeese. "We're actually entitled to three convictions."

"Three?" queried Harrelson.

"Um-hmm!" mused DeWeese as he drained his flask and restored it to its hiding place in his desk drawer. "One for robbery, one for murder, and one for pure goddamn stupidity."

11

Monday morning arrived—as it generally seems to do—much too soon. And with it came an even larger crowd of spectators than that which had filled the courtroom during the first day of trial. On this particular Monday, January 30, 1956—sixth day of trial in the Matter of the State of Ohio vs. Edward A. McMullen—there was not an open seat in the house. It was as though all of last week's attendees had influenced their friends, neighbors and acquaintances to come along with them to watch the final chapters play out. There was standing room only within the spectators' gallery, and precious little of that. Onlookers filled the aisles, doorways and even the windowsills in what seemed almost a frenzied attempt to view the participants and to hear the testimony.

After Judge Porter opened court promptly at 9:30, welcomed the spectators and laid down the rules which he would insist upon to maintain order, he nodded to the Messrs. Kerr and Dixon. It was, of course, their invitation to begin the presentation of the Defendant's evidence. Bill Dixon announced that their first witness would be the Defendant himself. Then, as Eddie McMullen made his way to the witness stand, Dixon gathered his papers, arranged them on the lectern reserved for the convenience of counsel, and scrutinized his notes. When both had assumed their respective stations, the Defendant's testimony began.

"State your name to the Court and jury," asked Dixon.

"Edward A. McMullen."

In response to Dixon's questions, Eddie McMullen told the jury that he was 29 years old, lived in Frankfort, Ohio with his wife Carolyn and his mother. He had, he said, lived and attended school in Troy from 1940 until 1941 or '42 when he'd quit school at age 16; then he'd driven a truck for his father who was a road contractor. He had also worked briefly for several other businesses in Troy, such as Troy Ice & Coal, Dutch's Service Station and Hawley's Taxi Company. Then in 1943, he'd moved "back to Greenfield" with his family and stayed with them until he'd married a New Carlisle girl in January of 1945 and resided there with her for all of two months, after which he'd returned to Greenfield. That marriage was formally terminated in January of 1947. His present wife, he said, was Carolyn, whom he had married in October of 1954. She was only sixteen at the time, and because her parents had not consented to their union, they'd traveled to Indiana, where the legal age was sixteen, and been married there.

Because he couldn't hide Eddie McMullen's criminal record from the jury, Dixon asked him about his short history. It would sit better with the jury he thought, if he laid it out for them on direct, rather than have the prosecution wring it from him on cross-examination. In his answers to Dixon's questions, the Defendant acknowledged that he had served in the U.S. Navy for "a little over a year, until November of 1944," when he received a bad conduct discharge for theft of another seaman's uniform. Then, in 1946, he was convicted of "B & E", breaking and entering, and was sentenced to the Ohio State Reformatory at Mansfield, Ohio, for a term of three to five years. He served six months of that term and then escaped, stole a car and fled to Roanoke, Virginia. As a result of that caper, he was apprehended and convicted in Federal Court on a charge of auto theft, and served a two-year term at Lewisburg, Virginia. After he'd completed that term, he was returned to Mansfield to serve a balance of thirty months on his original B & E conviction. He was subsequently paroled on that charge into the custody of Virginia authorities on yet another charge, that of unauthorized use of a vehicle, and was given a sentence of 12 months and fined $500. After serving two months on that charge he walked away (escaped) from a minimum-security penal farm, stole a pick-up truck and returned to Ohio. Directly thereafter, he was arrested for theft of the pick-up truck and extradited back to Virginia where he was again convicted and served part of a two-year sentence on that charge (although he escaped from that confinement on three separate occasions).

Upon completion of that short reprise of his client's criminal history, Dixon moved on to address the present charge. He segued into that subject by asking, "Now Ed, directing your attention to the twenty-seventh day of December, 1954, I will ask whether you worked that day?"

"I did. I worked in the shop with my father from eight o'clock in the morning until about 4:30 or 5:00 in the evening. We were repairing trucks and overhauling them so they'd be ready for the following summer."

"Where is your father's shop located?" asked Dixon.

"In Greenfield. Near the edge of town."

"Did you, at any time that day, go into the downtown area of Greenfield?"

"Yes, sir. I had lunch at Blackwell's Restaurant."

"Tell the jury," directed Dixon, "whether or not, on the morning of December 27, 1954, you saw and/or played cards with Glen Purdin."

"I did not."

"What did you do after you left work that day?"

"I went home to Frankfort, cleaned up and ate supper. Then my wife and I went to Rainsboro, Ohio; that's approximately 24 miles east of Frankfort."

"What time was that?" queried Dixon.

"Mmm," he seemed to be trying to remember, "It must have been sometime between 6:00 and 7:00."

"Where, in Rainsboro, did you go?"

"To the residence of Hope Thompson. She's my wife's sister."

"Did you see anyone while at Hope Thompson's residence?"

"Oh, yeah. My wife was there—and Hope Johnson—and Leona Knisely, I saw her."

"Who is Leona Knisely?"

"She's my wife's mother."

"Anybody else?"

"There were people in and out all evening. I just can't remember who all was there; they'd just come and go."

"How long did you stay there?"

"We stayed till somewhere between 9:00 and 10:00. Then we went home, watched some television and went to bed."

When asked whether he'd ever been in the Maddy residence, McMullen said he'd been there the first time in early January of 1955. It was after he'd been at Ada's bar drinking. He'd had too much to drink and he'd asked Cecil Maddy to let him out the back door where his car was parked. Then he fell down and vomited. Cecil helped him to his feet, told him he was too drunk to drive and insisted on taking him to his own home to sleep it off. Once at the Maddy residence, he found he was too sick to eat and Cecil and Ella Mae took him to their bedroom and put him to bed. When he awoke the following morning Ella Mae came in and told him to be as quiet as he could because Nick Valentine and Dorothy Newland were asleep in the living room.

The next time he was at the Maddy residence, he said, was in late January or early February of 1955. He told the jury that he and Cecil Maddy had been drinking at Ada's and they decided to go to Club 28. Eddie was in the driver's seat and they argued about whether he was too drunk to drive; he had insisted on driving and Cecil had accidentally slammed the door on the driver's side and mashed his finger in the process. Maddy took him home and Ella Mae had bandaged it. Then, he said, he and Cecil went on to Club 28 and stayed there perhaps half an hour, but finally, because his finger was throbbing, he dropped Cecil off at Ada's and went home to bed.

Eddie McMullen testified that during the time he'd been in jail awaiting trial, a period of some six months, he had been visited only once by his father, once by his mother, and not at all by his wife. By way of contrast, he told the jury that while he was in the Highland County jail in March of 1955 on a breaking and entering charge, he had been visited five times by Ella Mae Maddy, who had suggested that he implicate her husband in yet another breaking and entering charge then pending in Adams County, so that the two of them could run off together. On one such occasion, he said, she had put her arms around him and kissed him. He said that he had rejected her offer and her attendant demonstration of affection.

Finally, before releasing his client, Dixon asked a short litany of questions designed to present his client the opportunity to exculpate himself from the pending charge.

"Did you, on the night of December 27, 1954, give Glen Purdin a gun?"

"I did not."

"Did you ever see a pocketbook belonging to a man named Cleve Chipley?"

"I did not."

"Did you ever, on December 27 or at any other time, tell Ella Mae Maddy that you had shot a man?"

"I did not."

"Were you in Troy, Ohio on the night of December 27, 1954?"

"I was not."

"On the night of December 27, did you shoot and kill Cleve Chipley?"

"I did not."

And with that, Bill Dixon turned to Jim DeWeese and solemnly announced, "Your witness."

Jim DeWeese began his cross-examination by inquiring of Eddie McMullen whether he had forgotten about several other brushes with the law when he responded to Dixon's questions about his criminal record. He reminded the Defendant that he had been in jail in Hillsboro in August of 1946. And when McMullen acknowledged that he had forgotten to mention that fact, DeWeese asked him, "Do you remember why you were in the Hillsboro jail at that time?"

"On investigation," came the reluctant answer.

"Don't you know," persisted DeWeese, "that a charge of forgery had been filed against you and you were being held for grand jury action?"

"That's what I was being held for?"

"And prior to your having been in jail for forgery, had you been arrested for any other offense?"

"I might have been in on a traffic violation."

"Come on, Eddie, weren't you picked up in Washington Court House by the State Patrol and placed in jail for auto theft on or about July 27, 1946?"

"I don't know," McMullen answered. "I don't recall."

"Did you forget about that?"

Jim DeWeese had obviously done his homework. He knew more about the Defendant's past history than had been disclosed on direct examination. "Incidentally," he asked, almost as an afterthought, "after you escaped from the Ohio State Reformatory in Mansfield, stole a car and drove to Roanoke, did you go anywhere else?"

"I don't recall."

"Were you arrested in Roanoke for auto theft?"

"No, I was arrested in Birmingham, Alabama."

"Under what name were you arrested in Birmingham?"

"Burnell A. Smith."

"You used an alias?"

"Yes."

And, not surprisingly, DeWeese confronted him with yet other instances of his having been arrested, convicted and sentenced on additional charges of auto theft and of his having repeatedly escaped from custody. In fact, McMullen admitted, the last time he came home, in May of 1954, it was as an escapee from a Virginia correctional facility with a balance of a year and five months remaining to be served.

Before he left the subject of McMullen's criminal activities and imprisonments, DeWeese posed one final question, "Now, Ed, just so there will be no misunderstanding of your testimony, am I correct in that from the time you were arrested by the State Patrol on July 27, 1946, until May 5, 1954, when you returned to Greenfield as an escapee from Virginia, you were in almost continuous custody—in confinement on one charge or another?"

And because it could scarcely be denied, the answer came quickly, "Yes."

As anticipated, DeWeese then shifted his attention to Eddie McMullen's account of his visit to Hope Thompson's residence in Rainsboro, Ohio, questioning him as to times, activities and persons present. He ended his cross-examination with an extensive discussion concerning McMullen's account of Maddy's having closed his car door on his finger. In response, the Defendant indicated that the car was his own 1951, two-door Ford Victoria; that he had been situated in the driver's seat with his left arm hanging over the seat and his hand on the sill, when Maddy had slammed the door and caught his hand in the door "where it latches."

Not quite satisfied with McMullen's verbal explanation, he asked him to demonstrate his position and that of his hand and arm, using the witness chair as though it were the driver's seat of his car.

The Defendant's cross-examination ended with Jim DeWeese's somewhat perfunctory announcement, "That's all!"

Defense counsel then continued the presentation of its evidence with a series of five and ten minute colloquies with Eddie McMullen's family members and friends. The issues—from the defense standpoint—were *alibi*, whether Eddie McMullen was in Troy, Ohio or somewhere else that evening, and when and how did he injure his hand.

His mother, Eva McMullen, told the jury that she was positive that the injury to her son's right hand had occurred in late January of 1955, and yes, she was quite positive that it was his right hand. It had been bandaged for a considerable period of time. She also recalled that her son and his wife had been home all day on December 27, 1954—they might have gone out for a short period of time that evening, but she really couldn't recall that. When asked how she fixed the date in her mind, she was totally unable to grasp the question and ultimately failed to answer it.

Eddie McMullen's wife, Carolyn, was Hope Thompson's sister. She simply confirmed Eddie's own account of their activities on the evening of December 27, 1954 and his testimony as to when it was that he injured his hand. She did provide the names of more people she claimed to have been at Hope Thompson's home in Rainsboro that evening than had her husband, but apart from that matter, her testimony was almost a total reprise of that of her husband's.

Leona Knisely, Carolyn's mother, also claimed to have seen her daughter and son-in law at Hope Thompson's home on the evening in question. Hers was a large family, twelve adult children in all, and they were having a holiday gathering at the Thompson residence that evening.

Maxine Mercer and Hope Thompson, both sisters of Carolyn McMullen, also confirmed the presence of Eddie and Carolyn McMullen in Rainsboro that evening, as did the Knedler sisters, Joan and Betty, who were next-door neighbors to Hope Thompson and had stopped over to announce the fact that their mother had given birth to a baby boy that very morning.

The only other witness called by the Defense was Ralph Moyer, the service station operator who had, more than a year earlier, reported to Chief Hennessey that a young man had stopped at his home and inquired about a used furniture dealer. He was asked by Ellis Kerr to describe the man as best he could remember and then asked as to whether he could identify the Defendant as the man who had inquired of him that evening. Moyer attempted a description, but was unable to identify Eddie McMullen as the man he'd described. On cross-examination, Bill Dixon produced the police report containing Moyer's initial description of the man he'd seen that evening and demonstrated that the same differed considerably from Moyer's present recollection and did, indeed, describe the Defendant very well.

Apart from the Defendant himself, each of his witnesses' testimony, both direct and cross-examination was exceptionally brief. Ellis Kerr moved the admission into evidence of two exhibits, a birth certificate showing the birth of the Knedler child on December 27, 1954 and the Police Report of Ralph Moyer. Both were admitted by agreement, and the Defense rested its case at 10:35 Tuesday morning. Their entire presentation had taken less than a day and a half.

Because it was still early in the day—not yet time for the morning recess—Jim DeWeese promised the Court that his first rebuttal witness would be a short one, no reference to his height, he said jocularly, but to the time he anticipated his testimony would require. He then called to the stand a man, much taller than himself, named John Dunteman who identified himself as a private investigator, a 1947 graduate of Louisiana State University with a law degree; since his graduation he had been employed by a number of federal agencies as an investigator and as a detective. He had been retained by Mr. DeWeese, he said, to investigate the Defendant's claim of *alibi*, and in that context had interviewed Hope Thompson at her home in Rainsboro. In response to Jim DeWeese's questioning and referring to his notes, he identified several discrepancies in her testimony as to those persons who were at her home on the night of December 27, 1954, the time that Eddie and Carolyn McMullen had arrived, and the time when they left. The principal discrepancy arose from Eddie and Carolyn's testimony that they had eaten supper at home sometime between 6:00 and 7:00, then had gone to Rainsboro, some 24 miles distant, and Mrs. Thompson's having represented to him that the McMullen couple had arrived at her home at 6:30 and had dinner with her family at 7:30.

Ellis Kerr's cross-examination was brief, entirely perfunctory and totally fruitless. Judge Porter declared a brief mid-morning recess.

And no more than fifteen minutes later, Court was again in session and Bill Harrelson called the State's final witness to the stand. This was Charles Donaldson, the local Ford Motor Company Dealer. He testified that he was entirely familiar with Ford's 1951 Victoria Model, which was a two-door car and constructed in such a manner that passengers could access the rear seats through either of the two single front doors.

Harrelson then asked Donaldson to assume that the witness chair was the front seat of a '51 Ford Victoria and that he has sitting in that seat with his left arm, hand and elbow in the precise positions Eddie McMullen had described—and demonstrated—during Jim DeWeese's cross-examination.

"I can do that sir. In fact I replicated the position yesterday in a '51 Ford Victoria—and again this morning—just to be sure."

"Would you tell the jury whether or not, in such a situation it would be possible to catch your left little finger in the door when it was closed?"

"It would not be possible. The point of closure is well behind the driver's seat to permit access to the rear seat, and that clearance makes it impossible for a person sitting in the driver's seat as you described to catch a finger when the door closes."

On cross-examination, Ellis Kerr asked about Donaldson's attempts to replicate the event described by Eddie McMullen. "Specifically, sir, would it have been possible to catch your finger upon closure if you were in the process of entering the vehicle with your body turned and your feet still on the ground?"

The witness looked askance at Kerr before he answered. "Mr. Kerr," he said, "It would have been impossible to have closed the door with my feet on the ground."

And on that note, both lawyers released the witness. It was not yet noon, but all the evidence was in and the Court and counsel agreed to proceed directly to final argument and the charge by the Court so that the case might be submitted to the jury that same day.

Jim DeWeese argued the State's case and Ellis Kerr followed with his argument for the Defense; both lawyers contended that the undeniable weight of the evidence supported their respective versions of the events of December 27, 1954; both identified discrepancies in the testimony of the witnesses; and both acknowledged the State's burden of proving each and every element of the charge beyond a reasonable doubt. But the members of the jury had heard all the evidence and were quite capable of deciding for themselves whose testimony was credible and whose was not. Resolution of those questions, whom to believe, and what had truly been proven, was within the sole province of the jury. And upon completion of the arguments of counsel, Judge Porter proceeded to charge the jury as to the law to be applied and as to their duty to fairly and impartially decide the issues and to render a true and correct verdict.

At the close of his charge, Judge Porter explained the process they should follow in their deliberations and their balloting from time to time as their discussions mandated. He also explained that they would be provided with three verdict forms from which to choose. One such form was to be signed and returned if their verdict was that the Defendant was guilty as charged, the second form was to be returned if their verdict was guilty as charged, with a separate recommendation of mercy, and the third form was to be used if their verdict was that the Defendant was not guilty. He also instructed them that because this was a criminal case, their verdict, whatever it might be, must be unanimous. The charge was long, and as most such charges are, complex and prolix, but it had commanded, from start to finish, the full attention of the jurors and all of the more than 200 spectators who had listened attentively to every word. At precisely 4:00 p.m., it was finished and the jury was escorted to the jury room to begin their deliberations.

12

The moment the jury left the courtroom, the lawyers and Judge Porter convened at the bench to compliment one another on the manner in which the case had been presented, the civility which each had demonstrated and the capable professionalism which had characterized the entire trial. They were indeed professionals and had presented their client's divergent positions without displaying so much as a hint of sarcasm, incredulity or rancor. They agreed between themselves that there were no complex legal questions involved in the case and that the ultimate result—the verdict rendered by the jury—would depend on which evidence they collectively believed and which they rejected.

That exercise completed, they went their separate ways to await the inevitable summons from the bailiff to return to the courtroom to hear from the jury. Because the respective offices of the Messrs. Kerr and Dixon were located just across the street from the courthouse, it was agreed that they could return there to await the bailiff's call. Bill Harrelson elected to wait in Jim DeWeese's office just across the hall.

DeWeese entered his office first and was greeted by his long-time secretary, Helen Carstensen. She had followed the trial closely and had herself prepared most of the paperwork necessitated by the proceedings. But now, perhaps for the first time, she had a question. "Jim," she asked at her first opportunity,

"I think I have a fair understanding of this case and the significance of the wide discrepancies in the testimony, but I haven't been able to figure out why you've pressed McMullen so persistently on the subject of his injured finger. What real difference does it make how—or even when—he injured it?"

DeWeese and Harrelson exchanged querulous looks, before all three had seated themselves at DeWeese's desk. "I was afraid I'd lose you on that one," he admitted. " I just hope the jury works it out for themselves."

"I don't understand," she said. "Works what out?"

"Well," came the thoughtful answer. "I don't really know—and can't prove—how the little bastard injured his pinky, but I can sure as hell guess. I think that when Chipley pulled his own gun, McMullen tried to both push it aside and to shove Chipley away from him with his left hand. I also think that in the process, McMullen got his left hand in the way and shot the tip of his finger off by accident."

"And I think," chimed in Harrelson, "that Jim's 100 percent correct. The two events, Chipley's murder and the injury to McMullen's finger, coincided exactly—and I also think that's why he couldn't go to the hospital or a doctor. They'd have recognized it as a gunshot wound and reported it to the authorities."

"But..." began Helen Carstensen before DeWeese could interrupt.

"But we couldn't spell out that scenario to the jury in so many words," said DeWeese, anticipating her question. "We had no proof to support our conjecture; we'd have been guessing. And neither Kerr nor Dixon would have let that sort of thing go. We just have to hope that the jury will work it out for themselves."

They didn't have long to wait before being summoned back to the courtroom. At 6:00 p.m., just two hours after they had received the case, the jury requested a single additional instruction. In such a case, the jury is returned to the courtroom, as are the parties and their attorneys, not only to hear the question, but to hear the Judge's answer.

As a part of his original charge to the jury and his discussion of their choice of verdicts, Judge Porter had told them that if their verdict was that the Defendant were found guilty the Court would be required by law to sentence him to death, unless their verdict included a recommendation for mercy, in which case the sentence would be that of life imprisonment. The jury now wanted to know whether or not, upon their recommendation of mercy, there was yet a possibility that the Pardon and Parole Board could order his release during his lifetime. As soon as the question was asked and the implications grasped, an audible stir emanated from Eddie McMullen's family and the spectators who had remained in the courtroom. The question itself suggested the direction in which the jury was leaning.

Judge Porter responded by reading the statutory law of Ohio which at that time provided that in cases of persons serving a life sentence, the commission was required, after 20 years, to make a study and a recommendation to the governor. The commission was also required to make such a study and recommendation every five years thereafter for so long a time as the person remained a prisoner. It is the governor, he told them, who must ultimately decide whether the life sentence is to be commuted or not.

The jury then retired again and, less than an hour later, notified the bailiff that they had reached a unanimous verdict.

As soon as Court was reconvened, with all parties and counsel in attendance, Judge Porter asked the foreman, Paul Maxwell, to confirm that the jury had, indeed, reached a verdict.

"We have, Your Honor," responded Maxwell in a firm, respectful voice and manner.

"Please hand it to the Clerk," directed Judge Porter.

Then, as the verdict form was conveyed to him by Clerk of Courts Earl Mishler, Judge Porter instructed the Defendant to stand and face the jury. As he did so, he was flanked by his attorneys, both of whom rose and faced the jury. Judge Porter returned the verdict form to the Clerk and asked him to read it to the Defendant.

Earl Mishler was a tall, strongly built man, with a kindly, no-nonsense manner. In a clear, firm voice, he read from the form, "We, the jury in this case find the Defendant guilty of murder in the first degree, with a recommendation of mercy." He then "polled the jury" in the customary manner, calling each of the four men and eight women by name and asking of them, "Is this your verdict?"

When each of the jurors had affirmed their verdict, Judge Porter asked the Defendant whether he had anything to say before sentence was pronounced. Eddie McMullen made no audible response to the question, did not raise his eyes from the counsel table before him and simply shook his head.

Judge Porter then imposed the sentence mandated by statute, that the Defendant be conveyed by the Sheriff to the Ohio State Penitentiary and that he be confined there for the rest of his natural life. He next turned his attention to the jurors, thanked them for their service and declared that Court was adjourned, *sine die.*

Eddie McMullen had accepted both the verdict and his sentence stoically. His wife and his mother, Carolyn and Eva McMullen, had broken into tears and covered their faces as soon as the verdict was announced. They had had tears in their eyes since the jury had asked the Court for further instruction concerning the possibility of release in the future if there were to be a recommendation of mercy. Their emotional release may well have been tinged with relief that the jury had, at the least, not required the death penalty. That latter consideration was, as it happened, a very real one. The jury reported that there had been only two ballots, the first had been nine for conviction with a recommendation for mercy (life imprisonment) and three for conviction without such a recommendation (death sentence).

When asked by the press about the possibility of an appeal, the Messrs. Kerr and Dixon responded that they would need to confer with their client before that decision was made. Jim DeWeese and Bill Harrelson made no comments to the media; they simply observed the necessary amenities and retired to the privacy of the Prosecutor's office to celebrate their victory.

Theirs was a brief session. It had been a long trial, they had achieved their verdict and the Defendant had been sentenced. They were both physically and emotionally drained. Besides, it was well after dinner time and they were anxious to get home. Jim DeWeese, however, could not resist a final benediction. "Bill, he said, "I've been at this business a long time now, and I've always felt that we have, in this country, the finest system of jurisprudence anywhere in the world. It's not perfect; nothing ever is, but it's better than any other that we know of."

And when Harrelson nodded his agreement, DeWeese completed his benediction, "What we've just accomplished here these last several days, is a signal confirmation that the system, by God, actually works."

"Amen, brother. Amen," agreed Harrelson. "We did a good job and the system worked well, exactly like it's supposed to do."

Part Two

13

In all probability, Bill Dixon was more distressed by the jury verdict finding Eddie McMullen guilty of murder in the first degree than was the Defendant himself. Despite the compelling evidence to the contrary, Dixon remained convinced that Eddie McMullen was not within 80 miles of Troy, Ohio, at any time during the day or night of December 27, 1954. He strongly believed his client's protestations of innocence and in the *alibi* testimony that had been adduced at trial. He and his co-counsel, Ellis Kerr, filed the requisite motion for a new trial—which was summarily overruled by the Court—spent endless hours conferring with their client and consulting the legal authorities in order to somehow, some way, justify the filing of an appeal, but, in the final analysis, were unable to find any grounds upon which to base an appeal to a higher court. And, after much soul-searching and a thorough review of the Record, it was agreed by both lawyers—and the Defendant himself—that an appeal could not be justified.

In this context, it should be articulated that an appeal could only succeed if an appellate court were to find that the trial judge had committed some prejudicial legal error in his rulings at trial or in his charge to the jury or if there were insufficient evidence presented at trial to support the verdict rendered by the jury. And, of course, the lawyers could find no legal error committed by Judge Porter at trial, and there was certainly sufficient evidence presented—which, if believed—supported the verdict. In any event, there was no appeal filed and Eddie McMullen was transported to the Ohio State Penitentiary at Columbus to begin his life sentence.

Surprisingly, for a man who had admitted to at least four prior escapes from confinement, he turned out to be a model prisoner. During his years at the Penitentiary, he trained and played on the prison baseball team and he worked in the prison library, eventually attaining the post of head librarian. In many ways, he seemed better reconciled to his conviction and the accompanying life sentence than did his counsel.

And, while Eddie McMullen was serving his time, the world continued to revolve on the home front. The pending murder charges against Cecil Maddy were dropped shortly after Eddie McMullen's conviction. The Messrs. DeWeese and Harrelson determined that there was insufficient evidence of his guilt to warrant their proceeding further against him and he was dismissed pursuant to a *nolle prosequi*. Bill Harrelson announced that he would not be a candidate for re-election as Troy City Solicitor in the 1957 election, and Bill Dixon was elected to succeed him in that office. Ellis Kerr was appointed as Judge of the United States Bankruptcy Court in nearby Dayton and Jim DeWeese finally relinquished his Prosecutor's mantle in favor of William E. Kessler. All things local appeared to be progressing within normal, traditional and customary expectations.

During his service as Troy City Solicitor, Bill Dixon was involved with virtually every aspect of the local city government, and because he was an amiable and highly regarded young man, he very naturally developed a considerable rapport with virtually all the municipal officials and civil servants—including members of the local police force, with whom he consulted on a regular basis concerning traffic and criminal matters. During one such consultation, in March of 1964, he learned that a .38 caliber Colt revolver which the Bureau of Criminal Investigation had linked to the Chipley murder was still under lock and key at police headquarters—and had been kept there since well before the McMullen trial. Appalled that the existence of such a gun had not been disclosed to either himself or to Ellis Kerr prior to Eddie McMullen's trial, Dixon began to make inquiries concerning its provenance, and soon learned that the gun was one of four which had been recovered—in February of 1955—from one of three men apprehended after a burglary at the Braun Brothers Packing Company in

Troy. He also learned that all of the guns had been sent to the BCI at London, Ohio, where a series of ballistic tests were run and a report sent to Chief Hennessey to the effect that one of the two bullets recovered from Chipley's clothing had been fired from the Colt revolver. Then, in May of the same year, the gun and the two bullets were sent to the Columbus Police Department Laboratory for further testing; that procedure resulted in a finding that both bullets were fired from the same Colt revolver. A report of that finding was sent to Chief Hennessey, who investigated further and learned that this particular Colt revolver had initially disappeared from an Illinois penal institution and that Harold Bryarly, one of the Braun Brothers' burglars, had stated that he had obtained it some two years earlier from an unknown man.

Perplexed as to how to proceed with this new information, Dixon involved another Troy lawyer, William H. Thornburgh, who was not only a good friend, but one of the best trial lawyers in the county. The two of them brain-stormed and agonized over the best course of action available to them to rectify that which they both considered to be an egregious miscarriage of justice. Had Eddie McMullen's defense team been aware of this Colt .38—and the two separate ballistics reports—they might well have convinced a jury of the existence of a reasonable doubt as to his guilt and secured his acquittal. But that, of course, was history. Eddie McMullen had been tried and convicted more than six years ago; it was certainly too late for an appeal or for a motion for new trial on the basis of newly discovered evidence.

Ultimately, in September of 1964, they filed a petition for a writ of *habeas corpus* in the Supreme Court of Ohio, alleging that the State of Ohio had suppressed material evidence and thereby deprived the Defendant of a fair trial—and that, by reason

Bill Thornburgh

thereof, his conviction was a nullity and he was therefore being detained illegally. Because the petition for the writ alleged that the Warden of the Ohio State Penitentiary was the person holding Eddie McMullen illegally, it was the warden himself who was the Defendant in this new action before the Supreme Court which was, for that reason, styled *Edward A. McMullen vs. E. L. Maxwell, Warden of the Ohio State Penitentiary*. And, for the same reason, the warden was defended by William B. Saxbe and William C. Baird, respectively the Attorney General of Ohio and his chief assistant.

The case came on for trial before the Supreme Court in March of 1965—a virtual anomaly in and of itself, because appellate courts do not customarily conduct trials or evidentiary hearings. Proceedings in appellate courts are usually confined to legal issues arising out of the evidence adduced at the trial level; however, in certain special matters in which appellate courts have original jurisdiction, the testimony of witnesses can be taken and evidence may be introduced at the appellate level. Habeas corpus is such a special matter and Bill Dixon and Bill Thornburgh did, indeed, introduce both testimony and reports in support of their petition.

Specifically, they offered the official transcript of the 1956 McMullen trial and the testimony of Miami County Prosecuting Attorney James H. DeWeese and Troy Police Chief John Hennessey, both as on cross-examination. They also called two ballistics experts and introduced the London, Ohio BCI Laboratory ballistics report and the Columbus Police Laboratory ballistics report, both of which had been received by Chief Hennessey and forwarded to DeWeese well before the McMullen trial. And, upon the conclusion of all the evidence in this, the *habeas corpus* hearing, the Court heard oral arguments from both sides, concerning the existence or non-existence of an affirmative duty on the part of the Prosecution to have disclosed the ballistics reports to Defense Counsel prior to trial and, as a part of that consideration, the legal merit of Eddie McMullen's claims that he had been thereby deprived of his right to a fair trial and was therefore being wrongfully detained by the warden.

At the conclusion of the hearing, Chief Justice Taft complimented counsel for both the Petitioner and the Respondent on the presentation of their evidence and the eloquence of their arguments; he also expressed the thanks of the Court for the responsiveness of counsel to the several questions posed by the Justices and for the professionalism demonstrated by each side during the hearing. Finally, he indicated that the Court would render its decision in timely fashion.

Bill Dixon and Bill Thornburgh had driven together the 70-odd miles from Troy to Columbus for the hearing before the Supreme Court. Inasmuch as they had already spent countless days and hours together ferreting out the facts pertaining to the discovery of the "second gun," the ballistic testing and the experts' reports concerning it, and the ramifications of the Prosecution's failure to disclose it—and, of course, researching the law as applied in those few similar cases they could find in any of the now fifty states of the union—they had become mutually committed to their case and, at the same time, virtually inseparable. For that reason, if not simply as a matter of expediency, it was inevitable that they would travel to and from the arena together.

The return trip found the two young lawyers exhilarated by their exercise in the highest court in the State, guardedly optimistic of their chances for a favorable decision, and at the same time, relieved that this particular ordeal was over—at least for the nonce. They had done all they could do thus far and both considered that they had done it well.

"What do you think?" queried Bill Dixon as they made their way homeward on that chilly evening in early March. "Will they grant our petition?"

Bill Thornburgh had been about to pose the same question. He considered his answer for a moment, more for effect than for consideration. He had thought of little else since they'd left the Capitol Building. "About 50-50, I'd guess," he ventured, then, "Maybe even 60-40. *Habeas corpus* is always a tough sell, but if either of us is likely to ever get one, I'd think it would be here."

"My thoughts exactly," echoed Dixon. "But that could be wishful thinking."

"Maybe," said Thornburgh, "but if we don't win it here, I'm ready to re-file in the U.S. Supreme Court. I think our claim is that strong."

"If we can get into the U.S. Supreme Court," said Dixon. "That's always a tough challenge."

"Oh, I think we can get in alright," responded Thornburgh. "Remember this is a Fourteenth Amendment case, 'the right to a fair trial'. I feel sure we can get in on that particular constitutional issue. Remember *Gideon v. Wainwright*?"

"Oh, yeah, I remember it well," replied Dixon. "Maybe two years ago. But that was a 'right to counsel' case."

"Right on!" agreed Thornburgh. "And the Court got there by including Gideon's Sixth Amendment right to counsel, as a prerequisite to his receiving a fair trial, which they held to be a fundamental constitutional right under the Fourteenth Amendment, okay?" And when Dixon agreed, Thornburgh continued, "And I can't believe that the Prosecution's withholding of potentially exculpatory evidence would not, at the very least, raise a 'fair trial' issue, can you?"

"Makes perfectly good sense to me," said Dixon. "Let's hope we don't have to go that far. Let's just hope we win it here."

Jim DeWeese and John Hennessey had also made the trip to and from Columbus together. Their relationship, for the purposes of the current inquiry, had changed. They were not appearing as lead prosecutor and his principal witness, as they had at the trial stage, but rather as two subpoenaed, adverse witnesses appearing for the purpose of being cross-examined by Eddie McMullen's counsel.

As was the case with Dixon and Thornburgh, DeWeese and Hennessey also found themselves very much preoccupied with the day's trial proceedings and somewhat concerned about the Court's reaction to the evidence presented by McMullen's attorneys. DeWeese probably expressed more confidence than he actually felt, "I'll be very much surprised if the Court grants the bastard's petition," he remarked. "*Habeas corpus* is always a tough nut to crack. I can't remember more than a handful of cases in my own practice where a court, at any level, has actually granted one. Besides, the evidence against McMullen was so overwhelming that the jury convicted him on the first ballot. The only reason for the second ballot was to decide whether to fry him or let him off with a mandatory life sentence.

"And," he continued, "when measured against the trial evidence, and the jury's strong and unqualified reaction to it, it would be ludicrous to suggest that the Defendant's confused and tenuous 'evidence' could have possibly created a reasonable doubt as to his guilt."

"That sounds right to me," agreed Hennessey. "I will admit to you that I was a bit concerned at the time about holding back the second gun and the ballistic reports—and I guess I still am. At the same time, there was never any doubt in my mind that the verdict was correct. The son-of-a-bitch clearly shot Chipley and the evidence was irrefutable."

"You probably already know," he continued, "that Harrelson had misgivings as well. He kinda felt like we should have told Kerr and Dixon what we had, maybe shared the reports with them and let them do with it what they could. What he said was, 'if we didn't, it just might come back later and bite us in the ass.'"

"Well," mused DeWeese, "he certainly had that part right. Win, lose or draw, we have already been bitten. The question now is how bad we are gonna bleed."

A little more than three months later, the Ohio Supreme Court announced—and published—its decision in favor of the Petitioner, Eddie McMullen, and granted the writ of *habeas corpus*. In its written *per curiam* opinion, the Court recapitulated its understanding of the facts presented at the hearing before it, first as to how they pertained to the Bryarly gun obtained after the Braun Brothers robbery and the ballistics test results communicated to Chief Hennessey and to Prosecutor DeWeese. The Court then reviewed in detail the State's "strong circumstantial case" as shown by the evidence adduced against Eddie McMullen at his murder trial, including the polygraph results which indicated that he was, indeed, guilty of the robbery and murder of Cleveland Chipley, and finally, the Court alluded briefly to the Defendant's *alibi* evidence.

At last, then, the Court addressed the merits of the case from a legal standpoint by first defining the issue before it:

> *Petitioner bases his right to relief on the Fourteenth Amendment of the Constitution of the United States, which requires that no person shall be deprived of his liberty without due process of law. Part of the required due process is that an accused be granted a fair trial.*

Then, turning its attentions to the duties and obligations of the prosecution, the Court observed that:

> *Ordinarily, the prosecutor need only produce and present evidence which tends to prove guilt, relying on the defense to produce all exculpatory evidence. Under some circumstances, however, if the prosecutor becomes aware of evidence favorable to the accused he may have a duty to disclose it in order that the defense may be adequately presented.*

And that:

> *Whether the prosecutor has a duty to disclose evidence which is favorable to the accused and whether his failure to do so constitutes a denial of due process will depend on the particular circumstances of each case.*

And, again, quoting from a concurring opinion appended to an obscure Federal case:

> *It can be said that the prosecutor must not act in an essentially unfair way. But this is an area in which the question of fundamental fairness depends so much upon the facts of the particular case that a precise rule cannot be devised.*
>
> *It seems likely that many situations will arise in which a prosecutor can fairly keep to himself his knowledge of available testimony which he views as*

> *mistaken or false. But there are other circumstances in which a prosecutor must, or certainly should know that even testimony which he honestly disbelieves is of a type or from a source which in all probability would make it very persuasive to a fair minded jury.*

Finally—and predicated upon the foregoing considerations as applied to the specific facts peculiar to the case before it—the Court held that because the jury could have inferred from the excluded ballistics evidence that the actual murder weapon was not the snub-nosed gun borrowed from Cecil Maddy and that such an inference might have given rise to a 'reasonable doubt' in the minds of the jury as to Eddie McMullen's guilt. In sum, the Court found that he had been deprived of his right to a fair trial, granted the writ of *habeas corpus*, and remanded the petitioner to the trial court for further proceedings consistent with its findings.

"I read it," whined John Hennessey when he and DeWeese reviewed the decision, "and I think I understand it, but what's it mean in practical terms—without all the legal jargon?"

"In essence," growled DeWeese in obvious disbelief and chagrin, "it means that the Supreme Court just declared our trial and conviction of Eddie McMullen—nine and a half years ago—to have been a nullity. It's like it never happened. He still hasn't been convicted and the Court ordered his release from the penitentiary."

"What?" asked Hennessey. "You mean they've set him free? He just walks?"

"No, no, he doesn't walk and they haven't set him free. He's simply back where we found him ten years ago. He's still in the county jail, under indictment for murder. It's as though the trial never happened and he's been neither convicted nor acquitted. He'll just have to stand trial again on the same charge."

"But I thought the Court ordered him to be released," remarked Hennessey.

"The Court ordered that he be released from the penitentiary," explained DeWeese, "and remanded to the Miami County Court to await trial on the original charge. I expect his counsel will request bail, but I seriously doubt that Judge Porter will grant it. I don't expect he'll be on the streets until and unless he's found not guilty by another jury."

"How likely is that?" asked Hennessey.

"Not very, I would think," assured DeWeese. "Remember, we still have the same evidence and the same witnesses we had the first time around, and he was found guilty in exceptionally short order."

"But you're no longer the Prosecutor..."

"I know," acknowledged DeWeese. "And I'm really sorry about that. I'd really like to finish the job, send the bastard back to the Pen—or better yet—send him to the electric chair. That's still a possibility, you know. If he's found guilty again and the jury fails to recommend mercy, he'll automatically get the death sentence." He chortled at the prospect, "Wouldn't that be ironic? He could actually jump from the frying pan into the fire. That'd be truly poetic."

"But let's not worry about my not being able to complete the process," he assured. "Bill Kessler is an able prosecutor and a good trial man. He'll have the transcript of the first trial, the witness statements, and all the evidence—for both sides—with which to prepare for a re-trial.

He'll get it done."

The following Monday morning found DeWeese in a foul mood. He'd spent the weekend reflecting on the implications of the Supreme Court's decision as they pertained to him personally and was concerned for his own reputation. In re-reading the language of the decision—for perhaps the umpteenth time—it occurred to him that the general public might well perceive that the Court had felt that he had done something unethical; that his "failure to disclose" the existence of the Bryarly gun and the ballistics tests to defense counsel was in some manner improper or even 'shady' conduct, a perception that was wholly antithetical to his professional persona. "Goddamn it, Helen," he raged to Helen Carstensen, his long-time secretary and confidante. "It's not as though I didn't disclose the fact of the Bryarly gun and the ballistics reports to the Defense team. After I'd pressed the thing with Hennessey back in '55—before the trial—I got him to admit that he'd test-fired the Bryarly gun, exactly twice, and then he threw those two test-slugs into the same damn drawer he'd dumped the two slugs taken from Chipley's clothing in. He said he'd tried to mark the two sets differently, one from the other, so they wouldn't get mixed up, but he admitted it was 'remotely possible' that he 'just might' have sent the wrong set to the BCI along with the damn gun. He said he'd carved his initials into both sets—and then forgot which was which."

"I know..." began Helen Carstensen.

"Of course the BCI tests showed the bullets he'd sent them matched the gun he sent along with them," he groused. "They'd just been test-fired from it. In the final analysis, the damned ballistics reports were entirely worthless. All they really proved was that the test-slugs were 'very probably' fired from the Bryarly gun—which, in fact, they were."

"And, after I'd got all that from Hennessey, I told Bill Dixon about the Bryarly gun, the test-fired slugs and the mix-up."

"I know you did," said Helen Carstensen. "I was here, you know. I heard the entire story."

"Then you also know we talked about having Hennessey send the other set of slugs to BCI for examination... but finally agreed that whatever the result of that exercise, none of the tests would have any evidentiary value whatever—not at that point anyway."

" I remember," said Helen.

"So," DeWeese couldn't let it go, "we agreed to just forget about the Bryarly gun and the test slugs."

"Mmm-hmm," mumbled his secretary.

"And I guess that's exactly what he did," concluded DeWeese. "I really think he simply forgot all about it."

"Do you really?"

"Actually, I do. Bill Dixon is an honorable man as well as an excellent lawyer. I'm absolutely convinced that he wouldn't have deliberately set us up this way. In the heat of the moment, he forgot all about the Bryarly gun and our discussion. It's been more than ten years now and neither of us attached any significance to it at the time."

"But then, some two years ago," remonstrated Helen Carstensen, "when he 'found out' the Bryarly gun was still at the Department..."

"Eight plus years had passed, and it didn't jog his memory," concluded DeWeese. "And, in retrospect, the whole thing was my fault anyway. I should have made a formal written disclosure at the time. But I didn't, and that simple failure just came back to bite me in the ass.

"I told Bill Harrelson I'd take the heat for it."

"But you did disclose it," argued Helen.

"You and I know that, but I do not intend to argue about it at this time. The evidence is still strong enough to convict McMullen again," said DeWeese with finality. "I have been in the kitchen a long time now; I can stand the heat."

Bill Dixon and Bill Thornburgh could scarcely wait to visit their client and to bring him the spectacular news that his conviction had been held, by the highest court in the State, to be a total nullity. And Eddie McMullen was even more exhilarated by the news and upon his own perusal of the Court decision.

"I knew it would happen," he rejoiced. "After nearly ten years in this stink-hole, justice has finally been done. Hallelujah! I always knew the Lord would see that the truth came out—and the truth has set me free!"

His vindication was totally unrestrained. "You two guys have been great—and I surely do appreciate everything you've done. Thank you, thank you, thank you! You've both been the instrument of the good Lord. I just can't thank you enough.

"How soon," he asked eagerly, "can we get me outta here? Right now? Surely the Warden has seen this thing too.

"Maybe," he continued without pausing for breath, "you could swing by my mom's place on your way back to Troy this afternoon. I can't wait to give her the news, or to see her face. She never gave up on me; came to see me every chance she got—for nigh on to 10 years. She'll want to thank you too."

The two lawyers exchanged looks. Then it was Bill Dixon who tried to explain his situation now that the Supreme Court had ruled in their favor. "Eddie," he said in a tone that was designed to let his client down easily. "It's not quite that simple. You can't go home just yet..."

"Why is that?" Eddie McMullen interrupted. "It says right here that I didn't get a fair trial." He looked at the two lawyers quizzically. "I thought the whole purpose of the *habeas corpus* thing was to force the warden to let me loose. That's what you've been telling me all this time."

Bill Dixon laid his hand on McMullen's shoulder to calm him down. "Eddie, you need to read the order carefully. What it says is that you didn't get a fair trial and that, for that reason, the warden has no right to detain you— you've got that part right. But look at the last sentence, here where I'm pointing. It says, 'Petitioner should be remanded to the Court of Common Pleas for further proceedings according to law.'"

"Further proceedings!" Eddie stammered. "What the hell does that mean?"

Bill Thornburgh joined in the discussion. In eminently patient tones, he laid it all out for their client. "What it means, Eddie, is that it's like your trial never happened. It's a nullity. So you're back precisely where you were before the trial. You are still under indictment for murder and you're still awaiting trial on that charge. The order simply requires the warden to release you back to the Miami County Sheriff to be held until trial."

"What trial?" screamed Eddie McMullen. "You mean we gotta go through all that shit again? That doesn't make any sense. How many times do they get to put me through the meat-grinder?"

Both lawyers understood and empathized with their client's frustration. Bill Thornburgh tried to settle him down, "You understand Eddie, that because your trial has been declared a nullity, you haven't been legally convicted of anything, but..." he paused for effect, "you haven't been acquitted either. That's the reason they're gonna take you back to Miami County—to stand trial—a fair trial—on the original charge."

"But I've already served nine and a half years in this hell-hole on this conviction you tell me is a what? A nullity? How fair is that?" he pouted.

Bill Dixon interceded, "We understand how you feel, Eddie. It isn't fair. We all know that—yourself better than anybody. And we can't ever make it right—or fair. But we're well on the road to making it better than it was. We can't give you back those lost years, but if we can ultimately vindicate you, we'll at least have done all that's possible. And," he continued, "there does exist the potential that when it's all over, we may be able to get you some monetary remuneration from the State."

And before McMullen could respond, Bill Thornburgh added, "Think of something else, Eddie. First-off, we may be able to get you out on bail while we're waiting for trial—don't know if we can make it happen, but we'll try. More importantly, when it does come on for trial—and that should be real soon—the State will simply re-produce the same evidence we heard the first time out, no surprises there. But, we now have the ballistics evidence we didn't even know about before. We expect a prompt acquittal this time—and then it'll really be over."

"Okay, I get it," conceded Eddie McMullen reluctantly. "I guess I can stand to go through it again." And no sooner than he had finished that thought, another occurred to him. "Wait a minute," he blurted, "what about double jeopardy? I didn't think they could try you twice for the same crime."

"We've thought of that," answered Dixon. "But we don't think it'll work. Theoretically, you have not really been tried yet. Remember, the Court's ruling makes us treat that trial as though it never happened. But we'll certainly give it a shot—and we have some other ideas too. We'll see how it plays out."

Bill Dixon, Eddie McMullen, and Bill Thornburgh

14

It required no more than a few days for the lawyers and the Courts to finalize the necessary paperwork to enable the Sheriff to bring Eddie McMullen back to Miami County and re-book him into the jailhouse directly across the street from the Courthouse in which he had first stood trial nearly ten years earlier. He was actually back in residence in his former haunts before the end of July.

Then, true to their promises, on August 2, his lawyers promptly filed two motions with the Court: the first for the Defendant's release on bail and the second, for his dismissal from all charges based upon the State's failure to comply with Ohio's "Speedy Trial" statute which provided that:

> *No person shall be detained in jail without a trial for a continuous period of more than two terms after his arrest and commitment on an indictment or information, or, if he was in jail at the time the indictment or information was found, more than two terms after the term at which the indictment or information was presented, he shall be discharged unless a continuance is had on his motion or the delay is caused by his act.*

The two motions were argued before Shelby County Judge Huber A. Beery, in the temporary absence of Judge Porter, and just four days later, on August 6, he sustained the motion for release on bail, setting Defendant's bond

Senator Stephan Young and William E. Kessler

at $100,000. He overruled the motion for discharge under the statute, but set the case for trial beginning September 14 and ordered that if the State failed to proceed on that date, the Defendant would be released pursuant to the statutory speedy trial rule.

As it happened, though, it soon became apparent that the requirements for the drawing of a panel of jurors was such that the State could not proceed to trial on September 14 and the same was therefore continued, by agreement of all parties, to September 27.

Then, on the thirteenth of August, and at the request of Prosecuting Attorney William Kessler, the Court approved an order appointing Howard E. Swinehart, an experienced and talented local trial attorney, and also a former Assistant Prosecuting Attorney, as a Special Assistant to the Prosecutor for the McMullen trial. Three days later, Bill Dixon, who perceived a potential conflict of interest, tendered his resignation as Troy City Solicitor and procured an order for Bill Thornburgh to assist him in the upcoming trial.

And, at the last permissible moment, Dixon and Thornburgh served and filed their client's notice of *alibi*; Eddie McMullen, they claimed, was nowhere near Troy, Ohio on the night of the murder.

The stage, then, was properly set for Eddie McMullen's re-trial and the attorneys for both sides had but a short time for preparation.

15

Eddie McMullen's second murder trial began, as scheduled, on Monday morning, September 27, 1965, before a packed house. The re-trial of a man who had been tried and convicted nearly ten years earlier—and

H.E. Swinehart

had already served that same period of time behind bars—was a genuine anomaly. To the best of anyone's recollection such an event had never happened before, and that fact, coupled with the notoriety that the first go-around had engendered, had created considerable interest in the case, not only in Miami County, but in the entire State of Ohio. Many of those persons gathered within and without the Courthouse had attended the first trial and were anxious to learn how the re-trial would play out.

No one in attendance failed to realize that this second trial would likely be, for the most part, simply a reprise of the first. By the same token, however, it was also generally anticipated that there would be a number of significant differences in the crucial issues and in the testimony this time around.

The trial began before Judge Porter—again—with Prosecuting Attorney Bill Kessler and Special Assistant Howard Swinehart for the State of Ohio and the Messrs. Dixon and Thornburgh for the Defendant. The first two and a half days were consumed in the jury selection phase of the proceedings, in part because it became necessary to draw a second panel of seventy-five veniremen when the first panel was exhausted. Finally. Just before lunch on Wednesday, a jury consisting of seven women and five men was duly empaneled, sworn and instructed by Judge Porter.

Then, after the lunch break, the jury was taken, as before, to the Chipley residence to familiarize themselves with the general layout of the premises in order that they might better understand the testimony as it would be presented to them from the witness stand. Upon their return to the courtroom, Bill Kessler made a brief opening statement as to what the State intended to prove, and Bill Thornburgh responded on behalf of the Defendant. In his remarks to the jury, Thornburgh alluded to the fact that the Defendant had been tried for the same offense nearly ten years earlier and told them that he expected the evidence presented by each side would be essentially the same as before, except that the Defendant would produce new evidence that had not been made available to his counsel at the previous trial.

The first four witnesses for the Prosecution, Cleve Chipley's daughter, Mary Tooley, former police officer Virgil Cruea and County Coroner Bill Adkins rendered the same testimony they had given at the first trial; a fourth witness, Bessie Senior, the Stouder Hospital Records' Custodian, appeared briefly to authenticate the record of Chipley's arrival and the death certificate.

She had not testified at the previous trial, but her testimony added little or nothing to the total picture. At the conclusion of the Wednesday afternoon session, Dixon and Thornburgh requested a one-day continuance in order to "develop some further information that could not be procured over the coming weekend." After a short conference at the bench, Judge Porter granted the request. Trial would resume on Friday.

William Leffel, Chipley's nephew was the first witness to take the stand Friday morning; he was followed by Glen Purdin, Cecil Lee Maddy, and Ella Mae Maddy, all of whom had given damaging, inculpatory testimony concerning Eddie McMullen's appearance and activities upon his return to Greenfield the night of December 27, 1954, nearly eleven years earlier. Each of them testified precisely as they had before, and each of them again withstood a withering cross-examination by the Defense team. The jury listened intently to Purdin's repetition of McMullen's having asked him to return the pearl-handled snub-nosed .38 Colt revolver to Cecil Maddy, and his having done so; they heard Cecil Lee's disclosure that he had seen McMullen's bloody clothing containing Cleve Chipley's wallet and driver's license on the bathroom floor of his parents' residence, and his discovery of his father's pearl-handled revolver, containing three spent shells, lying on the bed; and most tellingly, they heard Ella Mae's testimony concerning the burning of McMullen's bloody clothing, the disposal of her husband's revolver in the creek, and Eddie McMullen's separate admissions to her that he had killed Chipley, in his own words, "It was his life or mine."

The final witness called by the Prosecution that day was something of a surprise. Marion Kendall, a resident of Troy and a construction worker, told the jury that, at about 5:30 on the night of the murder, Eddie McMullen and another man named Jim Abshire had stopped by his home. He said that McMullen was flashing a revolver, either a .32 or a .38, which he had said belonged to a friend of his named Maddy. He said that McMullen had taken the gun out of the pocket of his car and said, "I'm gonna knock off a bar or something, and I'll drop you off a case of whiskey."

On that note, Judge Porter announced that the day's proceedings were finished, admonished the jury, and wished them a relaxing weekend. Court was adjourned.

In much the same fashion as had become customary with Jim DeWeese and Bill Harrelson during the first McMullen trial, Prosecuting Attorney Bill Kessler and Special Assistant Howard Swinehart had fallen into the habit of retiring to the Prosecutor's office, still located just across the hall from the courtroom, to relax and to recap each day's proceedings—or, at this particular juncture—the entire week's proceedings.

"Well, Howard," asked Bill Kessler. "How're we doin' so far?" It was a rhetorical question. Kessler was well satisfied with the way the case was unfolding.

"Better, actually, than I'd expected," replied Swinehart. "I was a little concerned at first because we've lost some of the witnesses that DeWeese and Harrelson had the last time around, but I think we've managed to cover the ground anyway."

"Yeah, I know, but in ten years, we had to expect that. I think we're covered. We didn't really need Glen McConnell to authenticate the diagram, for example, since the defense stipulated to that. I'm sorry Della Chipley couldn't make it—her health simply wouldn't permit it—or Robert Leffel, he died a couple of years ago. It would have added an extra impact to have had their first-hand accounts directly from them—it would have been helpful to have the jury hear family members actually re-live the shooting from the stand." He sighed, "but it's not a perfect world and you can't have everything—especially after a ten year hiatus. I really hate the fact that Judge Porter won't let us use John Reid's evidence about the polygraph results..."

"And I don't understand that one at all," said Howard. "McMullen insisted on taking the test in the first place and then consented to its use against him. That hasn't changed—and the result hasn't changed either."

"I don't understand that one either," lamented Kessler. "And we both know it's not appealable. What really troubles me is the fact that we can't use Hennessey this time."

"I'm not sure I agree with you on that one. Sooner or later we're gonna hear about the Bryarly gun and the ballistic tests anyway. Seems like we might just as well put him on the stand and let it come out on cross-examination."

"No," said Kessler, with an air of finality. "If we call him, he's our witness and we're stuck with everything he says. If the Defense calls him, he's theirs and we can cross-examine him."

"And?"

"That gives us the chance to lead him along about the mix-up of the slugs. We couldn't do that on direct. I want him on cross. We can still get everything about his investigation from him before we try to explain the ballistics mess-up.

"I think we can get everything into evidence that DeWeese did—except for Della and Robert's testimony..."

"And the polygraph evidence." added Swinehart dourly.

"Yeah, except for that," Kessler agreed. "On the other hand, I think 'time and tide' has cost the Defense something too; I didn't see the names of all McMullen's *alibi* witnesses on their list. And, of course we've already sprung Marion Kendall on them and still have a couple more 'surprise' witnesses to spring on them."

"Surprise witnesses?" queried Swinehart. "I feel pretty sure McMullen has a pretty good idea what they're likely to say."

"No question about it," answered Kessler. "But I still think his lawyers will be surprised. I'm sure their client isn't telling them everything he knows."

"I'd bet on that," said Swinehart. "I'm sure they still actually believe he's innocent."

"Yeah. Well, he ain't."

16

Especially for lawyers in the midst of trial, weekends are much too short; paradoxically, they also seem much, much too long. On the one hand, there never seems enough time for the following week's preparations, while on the other, both teams are anxious to get back at it—to get their licks in, so to speak. Monday morning, October 4, did, of course arrive on time and the Prosecution began with the testimony of Charles (Bud) Hughes. Bud had spent nearly half his adult life in the Miami County Jail—usually for public intoxication, brawling, petty larceny, or some other minor offense. He actually seemed quite comfortable there and it was said of him that he actually committed his numerous petty offenses for the sole purpose of being re-committed time and again. After all, he'd boasted, it wasn't a bad place to live, warm in the winter, cool in the summer, three squares a day, a decent bed at night, room service as needed, free medical care, recreational facilities, television, and lots of companionship with others of his own ilk.

As an incident to his chosen lifestyle he met often with former police officer Jack Cheadle who had retired out of the police force and become Miami County's chief probation officer. Their meetings together were so frequent that the two had actually formed a sort of rapport, one with the other. And because Cheadle was known to have been one of the investigating officers at Eddie McMullen's first trial—and because the fact of Eddie's having to be re-tried on the same charge was well known to virtually everyone in the county, it was inevitable that the subject of the Chipley murder came up in their discussions.

And, in that context, and as a result of the rapport between Bud Hughes and Cheadle, Bud had revealed to Cheadle, in confidence, what he knew about the matter. Cheadle, of course had promised to keep what he'd learned in the strictest confidence, but was ultimately able to convince Bud to testify against McMullen, provided that he could be guaranteed immunity from prosecution as an accessory—or for anything else in connection with the events on the night of the Chipley murder. Then, when Bud agreed to do so, Cheadle led him to a local attorney in private practice, told his story, and an appropriate immunity agreement was negotiated and concluded with the Prosecution.

Now, on this Monday morning, Bill Kessler called Bud Hughes to the stand as his first witness. In response to the Prosecutor's questioning, Hughes told the jury that Eddie McMullen had, indeed, been in Troy on the evening of December 27, 1954; that he and Jim Abshire, a mutual friend from nearby Piqua, had come to his home and invited him to join them for a round of some of the local bars. He had agreed, he said, and the three of them, with McMullen driving, went first to a bar just north of town where they each had two beers and discussed the generally-known fact that Cleve Chipley, a local used-furniture dealer, habitually carried a lot of money on his person. He also told the jury of his having seen—and commented on—a pearl-handled gun sticking out of McMullen's belt. They had visited one or two other bars and, at the last stop, McMullen bought a six-pack to go.

Their next stop, according to Hughes, was at the curb on Jefferson Street, just around the corner from the Chipley residence. McMullen parked the car and got out, told Hughes and Abshire to stay in the car; that he was going to go see about a piece of furniture. He then walked to the corner of Jefferson and Madison and turned left toward the Chipley residence. No more than a few minutes later, he said he'd heard two or three shots fired and then saw Eddie McMullen running between two houses onto Jefferson. McMullen re-entered the car and drove "between 40 and 50 miles an hour" to the intersection of Water and North Market streets where he asked Hughes and Abshire to get out. The only explanation he gave was that he had to be back in Greenfield by eleven o'clock. Hughes said that he had noted that McMullen's finger was bleeding badly when he re-entered the car, but when asked about it, McMullen simply grunted a non-answer.

On cross-examination, Hughes admitted his own shoddy record of incarcerations for intoxication, forgery, probation violations and other repeated violations. He also acknowledged that he had been a cellmate of McMullen's since the latter was returned from the penitentiary in August. He acknowledged that he had been granted immunity from prosecution as a condition of his testimony, but denied that he had been promised anything else.

The Messrs. Kessler and Swinehart had expected to call Jim Abshire as a hostile witness to corroborate Hughes' testimony, but the subpoena issued to compel his attendance was returned marked "unfound." The Sheriff had been unable to locate him.

The two prosecutors conferred briefly before Bill Kessler formally announced to the Court, "The State rests, your Honor."

The defendant's counsel began their case with the same stale, almost sodden testimony, which had been offered at McMullen's first trial, i.e. the *alibi* witnesses, all of whom were offered in an attempt to show that Eddie could not possibly have been in Troy the night of December 27, 1954, because both he and his wife Carolyn had spent the evening in Rainsboro, Ohio—nearly 100 miles distant—visiting with Carolyn's family. This time around, however, the Defendant's *alibi* team had been nearly halved by reason of the absence of Carolyn McMullen, who was now divorced from Eddie, her sisters Hope Thompson and Leona Knisley, and a family friend, Joan Knedler, all of whom had testified at the first trial. There was no mention of the reason for their absence at this second trial. Of the initial *alibi* witnesses, only Carolyn's sister, Betty Mercer, and a family friend, Betty Knisely, actually testified that they had seen Eddie in Rainsboro that evening; Eddie's mother, Eva McMullen Pigot, appeared and testified that Eddie and Carolyn had told her that they intended to go to Rainsboro that evening.

Matters became more interesting Tuesday morning when the Messrs. Dixon and Thornburgh called former Troy Police Chief John Hennessey to the stand. Because Hennessey had been a key witness for the Prosecution in the first trial, his appearance now as a defense witness was something of an anomaly—not unanticipated, but nonetheless an anomaly. Because of the fact of his prior appearance for the Prosecution, the defense team was permitted to treat him as an adverse witness and to examine him as on cross. In response to their questioning, Hennessey acknowledged that a .38 caliber revolver had been recovered from a veritable arsenal of guns seized upon the arrest of three men implicated in a robbery at the Braun Brothers Packing Company in Troy some two months after the Chipley murder. One of the robbers, a man named Bryarly, had admitted that he had had the gun in his continuous and exclusive possession for the preceding two years. At Bill Dixon's request, Hennessey identified the gun—which he had been ordered to bring to court that day—by an imprint, which showed that it had once been the property of the Illinois State Penitentiary. It did not have pearl handles and it was clearly not snub-nosed; it had a full, standard, four-inch barrel.

Hennessey told the jury that he had sent the Bryarly gun, along with the two slugs found in Cleve Chipley's clothing, to the Bureau of Criminal Investigation in London, Ohio, and subsequently to the Columbus Police Department for testing and evaluation. Both ballistics reports were received by the middle of May, 1955, and both recited that one or both of the slugs submitted had been fired from the Bryarly gun. On further examination, Hennessey testified that he had turned over the gun, the slugs and the reports to Prosecutor Jim DeWeese in November of 1955, and that at a later date DeWeese had returned them to him with an instruction to keep them in a safe place. Bill Dixon asked that the gun, the slugs and the two ballistics reports be marked as exhibits and turned the witness over to Bill Kessler for cross-examination.

"How did you happen to come into possession of the two bullets, the two slugs, that were found in Cleve Chipley's clothing?" asked Kessler.

"They were given to me by Dr. Adkins, the County Coroner."

"And, upon receipt, what did you do with them?"

"I marked them with my pocket-knife and put them in a locked evidence drawer in my office."

"What other items did you customarily keep in that drawer?"

"Weaponry, mostly, guns, bullet casings, slugs, knives, maybe a blackjack, things like that."

"When you recovered the so-called Bryarly gun, did you cause it to be test-fired?"

"Yes, sir. I did it myself," answered Hennessey.

"How many slugs were recovered from your test-firings?"

"Two. I fired two shots and recovered both slugs."

"And what did you do with those slugs," asked Kessler.

"I marked them with my pocket-knife and put them in the evidence drawer."

"And then, if I understand correctly, you forwarded the Bryarly gun and the slugs recovered from Mr. Chipley's clothing to the BCI and subsequently to the Columbus P.D.?"

"Yes, sir. It was several weeks later."

"Describe, if you will, the kind of markings you made on the slugs with your pocket-knife."

"Well, sir, I tried to carve my initials on them, but it wasn't easy and I didn't do a very good job."

"On both pair of slugs? Those you got from the Coroner and those you'd test-fired?"

"Yes, sir."

"How were you able to distinguish between the two sets, one from the other—since you've told us you'd tried to carve your initials into all of them?"

"Well, sir," came the answer. "I've told you I didn't do a very good job with my initials; they looked different from one set compared to the other."

Bill Kessler put aside his notes and stepped away from the speaker's rostrum to approach the witness. "Chief, let me ask you if it might be possible that there could have been a mix-up of the two sets of slugs—all of which were in the same evidence drawer—and that you, or someone at your direction, could have inadvertently sent the two test-fired slugs, along with the Bryarly gun, to the BCI and to the Columbus P.D.?"

Hennessey shifted nervously in the witness chair before answering, "Well, I guess it's a possibility. I really hadn't thought about it before."

"Well, sir," pressed Kessler, "let's just assume for the moment that that's what happened, that the test-fired shells were mistakenly sent to the BCI and to the Columbus P.D., along with the gun from which they were fired, what would you expect the reports of their examinations to be?"

"Pretty obviously, they'd find a match," conceded Hennessey.

"Now then, Chief," Kessler wanted to get all he could, "in view of our discussion, would you agree that there is at least a reasonable degree of probability that that's exactly what occurred? That it was the test-fired slugs, rather than the Chipley slugs, that were sent to the examiners along with the Bryarly gun from which they'd been fired?"

The former police chief swallowed hard before answering, "Yes, sir. It's certainly possible."

"Probable." Insisted Kessler.

"I don't know," came the abject answer.

John Hennessey's testimony, primarily directed to the recovery of the Bryarly gun and the forwarding of that gun and the two slugs to the BCI and the Columbus Police Department for evaluation, had consumed more than three hours. The balance of the Tuesday session was consumed by the two ballistics experts and the introduction of their reports. Steve Molnar, Jr. was a laboratory technician with the BCI and officer Leroy Smith of the Columbus P. D. were both well-qualified and experienced as ballistics examiners—and the Prosecution conceded their qualifications. Each of them, on direct examination by Bill Dixon, explained to the jury the principles upon which the developing science of ballistic analysis and the matching of bullets and slugs with the weapons from which they had been fired were based, at least a part of which involved the test-firing of similar ammunition from a subject gun for comparison purposes. Having provided that short course on the subject, each of them separately described the tests and procedures which they had applied to the Bryarly gun and the two slugs provided to them by former Chief Hennessey and expressed their respective professional opinions that one or both of the slugs had been fired from the Bryarly gun. And, at the conclusion of the testimony of each of the expert's testimony, Dixon produced and offered the official written report that had been returned to Hennessey along with the gun and the slugs.

Bill Kessler's cross-examination of each of the two ballistics experts was essentially the same, both in form and in content. After a minimal clarification of matters touched upon in their respective direct examinations, he embarked on a series of questions which had already been suggested by his cross-examination of Chief Hennessey.

"Mr. Molnar, would you be good enough to describe for the jury the slugs that you received, along with the .38 caliber revolver, from Chief Hennessey?"

"Yes sir," the witness responded dutifully. "They were somewhat distorted in shape as a result of the forces applied to them, both from the firing of the weapon and from the ultimate impact with the target; they were readily distinguishable as standard .38 caliber in size and they appeared to have been separately marked with some sort of tool."

Bill Kessler retrieved the two slugs from the evidence table and handed them to Molnar. "Can you tell the jury whether these two slugs are the ones you examined?" he asked.

"Yes sir. I'm sure they are."

"You've told us that you received them from Chief Hennessey along with the gun. Do you know how he came to have them in his possession?"

"Not actually, sir. I know that he told me that they had been taken from the body of a murder victim; I think the victim's name was Chipley. But I don't have any first-hand knowledge about that."

"All right then," said Kessler. "Is it fair to say that you can express your opinion, to a reasonable degree of scientific certainty, that these two slugs were fired from the gun sent to you by Chief Hennessey, the Bryarly gun, but that you cannot testify that they are the slugs that were fired into the body of Cleveland Chipley?"

"Yes sir, that's fair."

"And, by the same token, you can't really tell the jury that this gun, the Bryarly gun, was the weapon that killed Mr. Chipley. Is that correct?"

"Absolutely. All I can tell you is that these two slugs were fired from this gun," he answered, holding up the gun in one hand and the slugs in the other.

"Assume, if you will, that the two slugs you have in your left hand were actually test-fired from the weapon you're holding in your right hand, and that both the gun and the slugs were then forwarded to you—perhaps by mistake—what would you expect your findings to be?"

"Only that the slugs were fired from this gun."

"It wouldn't tell you that the gun itself was a murder weapon?"

"No sir. All we can do is match the slugs that were sent to us with the gun—both of which we received from Chief Hennessey."

Bill Kessler was satisfied with the answers he'd received. "Thank you, sir. That's all."

And the day ended with virtually the same progression of questions and answers from Leroy Smith.

Then, the following morning, one of Carolyn McMullen's missing sisters unexpectedly appeared and corroborated the *alibi* witnesses' earlier insistence that both Eddie and Carolyn McMullen had been at her home in Rainsboro the evening of Cleveland Chipley's murder. Because he deemed further testimony in support of that story to be both tiresome and unworthy of belief, Kessler inquired of her no more than was necessary to convey his continuing skepticism and released her. And, on that note, the Defense offered its exhibits into evidence and rested its case shortly after ten o'clock.

Special Assistant Prosecutor Howard Swinehart immediately called Lynn Fisher, Jr. to the stand as the State's first rebuttal witness. Fisher, a tall, light-complected man in his mid-thirties testified that he and his father operated the Fisher Funeral Home in Troy and that he was present when Dr. Adkins, the County Coroner, removed the two slugs from Chipley's clothing during autopsy. Shown the two slugs that had been placed in evidence, he admitted his inability to identify them as those he had seen before. There was no cross-examination.

Swinehart then called a second rebuttal witness, a Thomas Brown, formerly a Troy resident and currently an inmate of the State Penitentiary in Columbus. Brown testified that he had first met Eddie McMullen at the penitentiary in August of 1964 when Eddie had asked him how he might get his hands on some of the tranquilizing medication that Brown was receiving in daily doses as a part of his psychiatric treatment.

"Did McMullen say why he wanted tranquilizing medicine?" asked Swinehart.

"He said he needed it be cause he 'had been in a bad way since he shot a dude'," answered Brown.

"'Shot a dude?'" echoed Swinehart. "What does that mean?"

"That's prison slang for having killed somebody," explained Brown. "It's been working on me ever since." And Swinehart let him go.

On cross-examination by Thornburgh, Brown admitted that he had spent all but 35 days of the previous 12 years in jail for issuing bad checks.

"Isn't it also true that you have actually been diagnosed by your psychiatrist as a pathological liar?" asked Thornburgh.

"Yes sir, that's true enough," Brown acknowledged. "But I've been under the care of the prison psychiatrist for quite awhile now and they've got me so I can control myself—what I've told you here today is God's own truth."

"That's all," snapped Thornburgh disdainfully, and returned to his seat at the counsel table.

Bill Kessler rose from his own chair and announced to the Court and jury, "That's truly 'all', Your Honor. The Prosecution rests its case on rebuttal."

Judge Porter informed the jury that they had heard all the evidence. There would be a short recess, after which he would instruct them concerning their deliberations and the law they must apply to the facts. Meanwhile, he admonished, for perhaps the twentieth time, that they were not to discuss the case with anyone.

Some fifteen minutes later, at precisely 11:45 that morning, the session re-convened and Judge Porter read to the jury that which was virtually the same charge he had delivered to a different jury in the same case nearly ten years earlier. Then, perhaps half an hour later, Bill Kessler and Bill Thornburgh argued their respective positions to the jury. Paradoxically, both of them demanded of the jurors that they "Do your duty." The panel of seven women and five men had the case by 1:20, right after lunch.

17

Bill Dixon and Bill Thornburgh elected to cross Plum Street to Dixon's office to await the summons from the bailiff that would bring them back to the courtroom in the event the jury had a question, desired further instructions or, best of all, had reached a verdict. Between the two of them, they had expended a great deal of time and effort in that which had amounted to a veritable crusade to exonerate their client and thereby finally win his freedom. In Dixon's case, it represented the culminating moment of a ten-year battle and was the more meaningful because he had persistently and devoutly believed in Eddie McMullen's innocence. Bill Thornburgh was not as firmly convinced as Dixon on that score, but had nonetheless given his all for the benefit of their client. It was ultimately the jury's call—not his—and for that he was thankful.

Time stands still for the litigants anytime a jury is out. No matter what the stakes may be, the existence of both apprehension and anxiety cannot be denied. And in the case of Eddie McMullen, the stakes were indeed high; a favorable verdict could set him free, while an adverse verdict could cost him his life.

At the same time, both of the two lawyers were guardedly optimistic. "The *alibi* evidence wasn't enough the last time," remarked Dixon, "but I think the *alibi*, coupled with the Bryarly gun does the trick this time."

"I think so too," agreed Thornburgh. "I'd imagine the jury would have to be impressed with the fact that the prosecution knew about it—and effectively hid it. That would just about do the trick all by itself. Then, too, the testimony and the reports of the experts was eminently persuasive and virtually incontrovertible."

"Unless the jury buys into Kessler's suggestion that John Hennessey sent them the test-fired slugs by mistake," cautioned Dixon.

"They're not gonna buy that fairy tale," Thornburgh insisted. "It's too obvious a red herring; it's just not credible."

Bill Kessler and Howard Swinehart didn't have to leave the building to await word from the bailiff. They had simply walked across the hall to the Prosecutor's office, where they removed their jackets, loosened their ties and relaxed. While they too felt the inevitable anxiety that typically accompanies their enforced vigil, both of them felt an abiding confidence in the final outcome, and neither of them expected a long wait. "Less than three hours," Kessler guessed.

"Now that's optimistic," appended Swinehart. "I'll give them another hour. We'll see."

"They did it in three last time; shouldn't take any more this time."

"Hope you're right," said Swinehart. "It'd be good to be home by suppertime. By the way, that was a nice job on Hennessey and the two ballistics guys. I think the jury got the message on that one."

"Thank you," said Kessler acknowledging the compliment. "I don't see how the jury can reconcile the evidence any other way. There sure as hell can't be any doubt the son-of-a-bitch was in Troy that night, so his *alibi* is gone. That makes a liar out of him and the jury simply needs a way to explain away the ballistictitians—if there is such a word. I think we showed them the way."

Even though they were no longer involved, both Bill Harrelson and Jim DeWeese had followed the case closely. Now they had slipped unobtrusively into the Prosecutor's office to wait out the jury verdict. "Ballistictitian?" echoed DeWeese. "Where the hell did that come from? Is that anything like a tactician?"

"Or maybe a statistician?" suggested Harrelson.

"Hell if I know," admitted Kessler. "I just made it up, so it's my word. And I can do whatever I want with it. I might even copyright it. Where'd you two bozos come from?"

"The courtroom," answered DeWeese, "like everybody else in the county. We wanted to make sure you two yahoos didn't screw this thing up."

"And?" asked Swinehart.

"We took a vote and decided you did okay—but it was close," said Harrelson.

"You did a nice job of contending with the ballistic screw-up," DeWeese volunteered. "The jury had to be able to figure that one out."

"Ballistictitians, ballistictitians," corrected Swinehart. "Remember it's his word."

"I was afraid to use it," said DeWeese. "He said he was gonna copyright it. It's just a damn shame the real murder weapon, the pearl-handled job, never showed up. Any word on that?"

"Actually," said Bill Kessler, serious again, "we did get word that some redneck recluse over in 'Sotty' County claims he's got the damn thing—pearl-handles, short barrel—but he wouldn't give it up, or even let us see it. Said he'd use it on anybody who tried to get it away from him."

"'Sotty' County?" queried Bill Harrelson. "Where the hell's that?"

"Scioto County," supplied Kessler. "Sotty County's what our informant called it. We asked the Sheriff over there to check it out, and he flat refused. Said he knew this old coot meant business and he wasn't gonna let any of his deputies get all shot up on a whim—or a rumor."

And at that point, the jury buzzer rang, and a moment later the bailiff stopped by the office. "Jury's back. They've got a verdict."

Despite Judge Porter's stern warning to the overflowing audience in his courtroom that there were to be no demonstrations, a considerable number of audible gasps and expressions of consternation made their way through the crowd when Clerk of Courts Earl Mishler read the "Not Guilty" verdict handed to him by the jury foreman, Robert Putnam. Above the rising din of protestations, Mishler polled the members of the jury and each member affirmed that he or she had agreed with, and signed, the verdict.

The Defendant, Eddie McMullen, who had been ordered to stand and face the jury while the verdict was being read and the jury polled, barely changed his expression. He remained standing, staring stoically ahead as Judge Porter thanked the jurors for their service, ordered Eddie to be discharged from custody, and declared an adjournment.

Moments later, on the outside courthouse steps, flanked by his counsel and surrounded by newspaper reporters, he did smile briefly. "I'm very happy," he told them. "And I want to thank the jury for the true justice I should have received 10 years ago. Although I regret the time I spent at the penitentiary, they were, for me, very important years, and I want everybody to know that I truly hold no malice or animosity toward anyone."

His mother, Eva Pigot, told the reporters, "Now I believe there really is a God in Heaven. I've been through this ordeal twice now, and I'm glad it's finally over."

The two pair of Prosecutors, Kessler and Swinehart, and DeWeese and Harrelson, had re-convened in the prosecutor's office where they shook their heads in shock and dismay, each of them separately trying to fathom what must have run through the jurors' minds. Their former confidence dashed and their jocularity entirely dissipated, they were virtually in a state of shock.

"I simply can't believe it," stammered Swinehart. "Three hours! It took them less than three hours to fuck this thing up."

Bill Kessler just leaned back in his swivel chair and pivoted from side to side. "The only thing I can think of is that they couldn't link the damn Bryarly gun to McMullen. They must have believed that was the murder weapon and they couldn't tie it to him."

He slapped his desk blotter with his open hand and added, "Goddamit! I tried to tell them every way I could that Hennessey mixed up the damn slugs; I don't know how I could have made it any clearer."

"Neither do I, Bill," said Swinehart. "I think we just have to blame it on the system; it doesn't always work like it's supposed to do."

An hour or so later, after the consolation gathering had ended, Bill Harrelson walked down the courthouse steps with Jim DeWeese. "I think Howard had it right," he said. "The system doesn't always work."

"I'm sure you're right," DeWeese agreed. "The system failed this time."

"I remember," said Harrelson, "ten years ago, you told me you thought ours was the best legal system in the world..."

"I did," DeWeese interrupted. "And I still do. Ninety-nine times out of a hundred we come up with the right answer, and that's not a bad average. But remember that no matter how perfect or well-designed the system, it's still operated by human beings. And human beings are fallible; we make mistakes. And that's when the system fails. We just saw it happen."

Bill Thornburgh, Bill Dixon, Eddie McMullen, Eva Pigot and Guy Pigot

AUTHOR'S NOTE

I personally had the opportunity to watch most of Eddie McMullen's first trial in 1955. I can still see Bill Harrelson being hooked up to John Reid's polygraph machine in order that the jury might better understand how it recorded the body's physiological reactions when providing an untruthful answer and his unsuccessful attempts to fool it. He couldn't. By the same token, my own experience tells me that it too, like our system of jurisprudence, is not totally infallible.

Just prior to the second trial, I was the attorney to whom Jack Cheadle brought Bud Hughes for the purpose of negotiating a guarantee of immunity in exchange for his coming forward and testifying against McMullen. I had a full account from him of his activities—and those of Eddie McMullen—that evening, and I have never had reason to doubt that his account was entirely truthful. He asked only that he be assured immunity from prosecution, nothing else. There were no promises of early release or special consideration. He had simply lived with it for longer than he could and wanted to get it off his chest.

Then again, I had the chance to follow the second trial, though not so closely as I had the first. I did make it a point to hear Bud Hughes' testimony and can confirm that he told the jury precisely the same story he had told me. I believed him.

I understand that Bill Dixon has never wavered in his belief in his client's innocence. With all due respect to that very fine, persistent and perceptive lawyer, I cannot agree.

Shortly after his acquittal of Cleve Chipley's murder, there was a suggestion from Bill Thornburgh that Eddie McMullen was considering the filing of a claim against the State of Ohio to compensate him for the time he'd spent in prison. That never happened; no such claim was ever filed.

That which did happen was that in March of 1971, Eddie McMullen filed, *pro se*, a motion for the issuance of an order requiring the State of Ohio to remove, or cause to be removed, from the files and records of the Ohio Penitentiary, the Bureau of Criminal Investigation and Identification, the Department of Mental Hygiene and Correction, and the Pardon and Parole Commission, any and all records acquired as a result of, or in any way pertaining to, his detention and imprisonment for the period beginning February 3, 1956 through July 22, 1965. The motion was summarily denied by the Honorable John M. Kistler, who was then Judge of the Common Pleas Court of Miami County. The truly intriguing aspect of that small foray is that the motion recites that the Defendant "...is now incarcerated in the Ohio Penitentiary, on other charges not connected with his commitment from Miami County."

ACKNOWLEDGMENTS

In my attempt to recreate the ten-year saga of Eddie McMullen's travails through the court system—along with those of the other participants—I have had the benefit of Bill Dixon's copy of the transcript of the witnesses' testimony in the first trial (because the second trial resulted in an acquittal from which no appeal would lie, no such transcript exists for that event). In that regard, I very much appreciate the accommodation of both Bill Dixon, and his son, the Honorable Greg Dixon, who is presently Judge of the Probate Division of the Common Pleas Court of Miami County. I have also benefitted from my separate conversations with former Prosecuting Attorney (and later Judge) Bill Kessler, former Court Reporter Eleanor Barringer, who faithfully recorded the proceedings of the second trial, and most especially, Bill and Pat Leffel, who were more than gracious in sharing with me their separate recollections of the events of Cleve Chipley's murder and Eddie McMullen's two trials; my sincere appreciation to all.

CARS

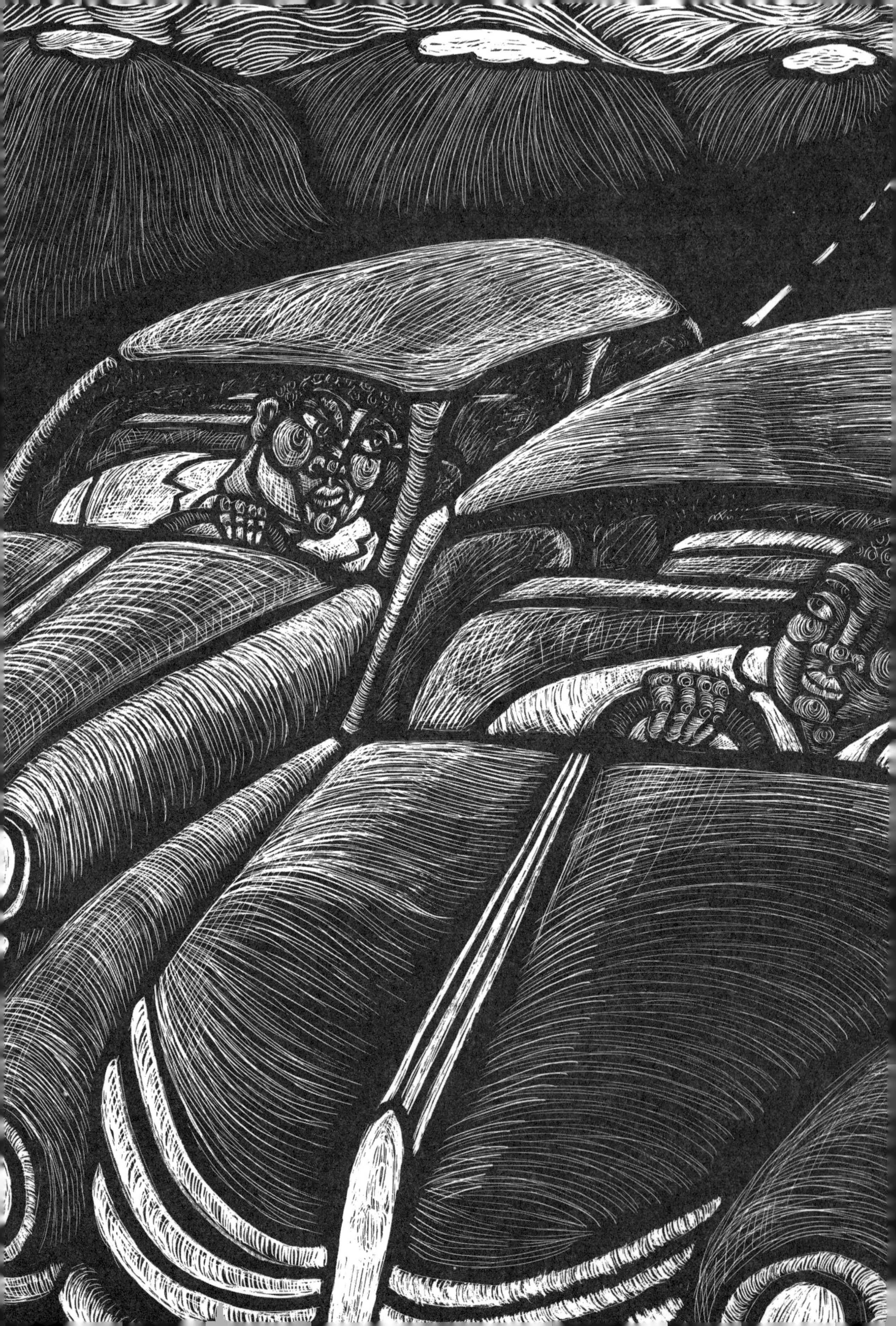

1

Not yet 25 years old in September of 1951, Tom Druley had already developed a healthy work ethic. Although he held a steady daytime job with a construction company, he had answered a newspaper ad and procured a nighttime job with the Irvin-Deeter Funeral Home on South Cherry Street in Troy, Ohio. Opportunities for work of that sort were plentiful, if not particularly desirable, partly because of the long, lonely hours, and partly because of the seemingly macabre business of working with the remains of human beings who had, for one reason or another, departed from life. Because the town had no regular ambulance service and emergency medical squads and technicians were as yet a thing of the future, and because the hearses owned by the local funeral parlors were generally available for the transport of sick or injured persons (without charge, of course; the initial provision of ambulance service often led to the later—and more lucrative—provision of funeral services), the principal responsibility of a funeral home's night-man was to await, and to respond to, emergency calls for ambulance services. Clearly the job also entailed other responsibilities, janitorial, handyman, and occasionally prepping a corpse for embalming, but the answering of emergency calls and the provision of patient transport was primary.

Actually, Tom rather enjoyed the job. The workload was light, especially after an eight-hour day of heavy construction work, and the occasional emergency run provided a welcome diversion from his customary work routine. Besides, he had met—and subsequently married—an attractive young nurse he'd met on just such a run to the local hospital a couple of years earlier.

Shortly after 10:45 on the evening of September 20, 1951, he received a call from Miami County Sheriff Richard Seifried informing him that an ambulance was required on Route 25, about a mile north of the city limits. "There's been a bad accident, car's in the ditch, and the driver needs transport to the hospital as soon as possible. I can't tell you whether he's dead or alive, but he's pretty bad off."

"Be right there," said Druley. "Five minutes, tops."

He wouldn't admit it, even to himself, but the Sheriff's call had been a welcome relief and added just the least bit of spice to an otherwise uneventful evening. He pulled up the overhead garage door, started the engine of the Home's shiny black hearse, activated the emergency lights and made the short run up the highway well within the promised five minutes. He had no difficulty locating the scene; blinking red and white lights from the Sheriff's cruiser, along with a battery of spotlights, illuminated the entire area. Sheriff Seifried met him on the highway and led him to the remains of a severely damaged automobile. "Victim's still in the car," he said. "Looks like he lost control—maybe blew a tire or something—went off the road, knocked down three or four of those concrete posts and a handful of advertising signs, then hit the ditch pretty hard."

"Wow!" said Druley, "Looks like he must've been movin' right along."

"Sure does," responded Seifried. "There's a solid steel core in the center of each of those concrete posts and he sheared 'em all off at ground level. Better get him to the hospital as soon as you can. I'll have my deputies help you."

Despite the heavy damage to the vehicle, the driver was easily extracted from the wreckage. Tom Druley had brought a stretcher down into the ditch where he and the deputies managed to place the driver's inert form onto it and carry it up the steep bank to the hearse. As soon as the injured man was aboard and properly secured, Tom took off for Stouder Memorial Hospital. As it happened, there was no need for undue haste. The man, still unidentified, was pronounced "dead on arrival."

"Might as well just take him down to your place, Tom," said the doctor on call. "Clean him up as best you can and keep him cool. I expect the Sheriff will want to sort it all out in the morning."

Tom Druley had been on the funeral home job for several years and was fully familiar with the drill. As soon as he'd conferred with Seifried and arranged for a deputy to assist him, he returned—at a more leisurely pace—to the funeral home, where he parked the hearse in the garage and, assisted by the deputy, had the man laid out on a steel trolley in the embalming room. Then, by way of respite from their labors, Druley and the deputy viewed the dead man. They learned from his driver's license that his name was Ben Sain, aged 24, and his residence was in nearby Sidney. He was a good-looking black man, perhaps six feet in height, athletically built and well-dressed with few, if any, obvious injuries. There were no bruises, lacerations and no signs of bleeding to be seen.

"I don't see a mark on him," remarked the deputy. "What d'ya think killed him?"

"Can't imagine," replied Tom. "Heart attack, head trauma, broken neck, maybe. Hard tellin'. I'll clean him up tonight, get him ready for Mr. Deeter. We'll know more tomorrow." The deputy said he'd follow-up the next day and bid Tom goodnight.

"See you then," said Tom. "Thanks for the help. This guy was heavy; probably 200 pounds."

As soon as he was alone with the deceased man, Tom wrapped himself in an apron and wrested the man's clothing off his body. He had expected blood and other body fluids, but found none. He had also expected evidence of severe trauma, but found no bruises, broken bones or other indication of serious bodily injury. He shrugged, and set to the work of cleaning him up preparatory to Norm Deeter's embalming procedures in the morning. "Never can tell," he muttered to himself, "Coulda been a heart attack, but, at his age, it doesn't seem likely. Hard to believe he coulda done that much damage to the car—and those concrete posts—without beatin' himself up, too."

Then, of course, he found it. A little tiny hole, about a quarter inch in diameter in the man's left temple. No blood, just an unexplained, wart-sized hole, almost invisible because of the young man's dark, thick hair.

Tom stopped his cleansing activities and telephoned the Sheriff's office. "Sheriff Seifried," he said into the phone, "I think you might wanna' stop over here and see what I've found. I'm not sure this guy was killed in an auto accident."

"Be right there, Tom," replied Seifried. "And it sounds like maybe I'd better have the coroner come too?"

"I think that might be a good idea," came the nervous response.

Within a matter of minutes, Sheriff Seifried had walked the block and a half from his office to the funeral home, and not more than ten minutes later County Coroner Charles Kiefer joined them. "Looks for all the world like a bullet hole to me," remarked Kiefer. "Mighta been some kinda sharp instrument, but I think we'll find a bullet in there."

"But there's no blood," interjected Seifried. "Not in the hair around the wound, not on his clothes—not even in the car, best we could tell."

"I think he was killed instantly, Dick—by a bullet to the brain—and remember, dead men don't bleed; the heart stops, blood flow stops, too," said Kiefer. "I'll order an autopsy in the morning." Then, he looked to Druley and said. "Leave him be, Tom, right where he is, 'till after the autopsy. Sheriff'll tell you what to do then. Okay?"

"Yes sir," said Tom. "I'll make sure nobody touches him."

"Good thing you found that little bitty hole, Tom," Seifried remarked. "We missed it and if you or Norm had missed it too, nobody'd have ever known."

The discovery of that which appeared to be a bullet hole in the dead man's head led to further investigation by Sheriff Seifried, Coroner Kiefer, and members of the State Highway Patrol throughout the remainder of the evening and into the early morning hours of September 21. They found a bullet hole in the driver's side door of the wrecked automobile and that which looked like a .22 caliber slug, which appeared to have penetrated the car door, pierced the rolled-down window and lodged itself in the interior wall of the door.

From their interviews with witnesses and telephoned reports to the sheriff's office, the officers were able to piece together a working hypothesis as to what had occurred and who might have been involved. They were first able to ascertain that the dead man was named Ben Sain, that he was 24 years old, had moved to Sidney, Ohio, from Forest City, Arkansas some four years earlier and had resided there with a cousin, Robert Sims. He had been employed at the George Stamm Garage in Sidney and was reputed to be an excellent mechanic. On Thursday, September 20, he had borrowed a car from a friend and driven to Troy where he picked up another friend, Preston Lewis, and two girls, Joanne Clay and Jeanette Ewing. From there, the two couples traveled to Sidney to "do the town"; then after a couple hours Sain had returned his three guests to their homes in Troy and prepared to return to Sidney. He stopped for gas at "Zwiebel's Corner", a popular gathering place at the corner of Main and Elm, where he was accosted by a Cecile Huggins, a 24-year-old Troy man, with whom Sain had carried on a running argument over a young girl for the past year or more. It seemed that the argument had heated up and worked its way across Elm Street, the two men pushing and shoving one another, to a company parking lot, where Sain slapped Huggins and Huggins hit Sain with a rock, before some of the onlookers broke it up.

The fight seemingly over, Sain retrieved his friend's car, paid for the gas and started up the Dixie Highway, Route 25, for Sidney. Meanwhile, the officers speculated, Huggins had run to his home on nearby Madison Avenue, availed himself of the family car and a handgun of sorts, and pursued Sain up the Dixie. He had apparently caught up with him a mile or so out of town, pulled alongside and fired two shots into the Sain automobile, one of which had pierced the driver's side door while the other had buried itself into Sain's left temple and killed him instantly. Directly thereafter, the driverless car had sheared off the concrete posts along the right side of the highway and landed in the ditch. The officers' hypothesis was more or less confirmed when they returned to the Sheriff's office and learned of a report from a southbound truck-driver who had seen the two automobiles speeding up the highway in the northbound lane, and was subsequently passed by one of the two as it headed back towards town.

Their hypothesis was further confirmed Friday afternoon when Doctors B.M. Hogle and William N. Adkins, Assistant County Coroner, reported that they had conducted an autopsy and found a bullet, presumably a .22 caliber slug, in Ben Sain's brain. Death, they agreed, would have been instantaneous; they also speculated that Sain had immediately slumped sideways onto the passenger seat and thereby avoided further obvious injury.

That same afternoon Sheriff Seifried went to the nearby Aeroproducts plant, where Cecile Huggins was known to be employed. He was advised, however that Huggins had left the plant at 3:00 p.m. Then, an hour later, he was found at his home by Patrolmen Harold Wagner and Paul Kessler and placed into custody without incident. "I heard you guys might be lookin' for me," he said nonchalantly. He was told that he would be held for investigation concerning the murder of Ben Sain the previous evening, but made no statement concerning his guilt or innocence.

2

By Friday evening, Ben Sain's body had been released, embalmed and prepared for viewing at the Irvin-Deeter funeral home. A surprising number of friends made the trip from Sidney for that event, including Sain's employer, Roy Ingersoll, of Stamm's Garage. The consensus was that Sain had been a talented mechanic and was well-regarded by all who knew him. The following morning, Saturday, his body was shipped back to Arkansas, where he had been born and raised.

Also, on Saturday morning, Cecile Huggins, not yet represented by an attorney, admitted that he and Sain had had a fight over a woman Thursday evening, but denied that he had shot and killed the man and claimed he had not been anywhere near the North Dixie Highway that entire day. He also insisted that he had an *alibi*, but declined to elaborate.

Meanwhile, Sheriff Seifried was frustrated in his efforts to procure a search warrant of Huggins' residence—specifically for a handgun—by the absence of both County Prosecutor James H. DeWeese and Common Pleas Court Judge David S. Porter. His deputies had found a number of .22 caliber cartridges in the Huggins family car, but had not located a weapon. And, despite the fact that no formal charge had yet been filed, an arraignment before Justice of the Peace Leo Gross was scheduled for the following Monday at 10 a.m.

Then, first thing Monday morning, and precisely as anticipated, an affidavit was filed by Robert D. Sims of Sidney, Ben Sain's cousin, charging that "on September 20, 1951, one Cecile G. Huggins unlawfully, purposely and deliberately and of premeditated malice did kill Ben Sain contrary to the section 12400 of the Ohio General Code": first degree murder.

The statute referenced in the charge specifically provided that:

> *Whoever, purposely and of deliberate or premeditated malice...kills another is guilty of murder in the first degree and shall be punished by death unless the jury trying the case recommends mercy, in which case the punishment shall be imprisonment in the penitentiary for life.*

Troy attorneys Harley D. Enyeart and William M. Dixon were on hand in Justice Gross' office to represent the prisoner when he arrived in the custody of Sheriff Seifried and Chief Deputy Robert Henning. The State was represented by Prosecuting Attorney James H. DeWeese. Huggins showed no emotion at the time and answered with a mild, "Not guilty," when asked how he pled to the charge. At Enyeart's request, a preliminary hearing was scheduled for the following Friday at 1 p.m., and Huggins was returned to the county jail.

Directly after the arraignment, Sheriff Seifried was finally able to get his search warrant for the Huggins home and the family car. His search turned up a .22 caliber target pistol, which was owned by Cecile's younger brother, Robert Huggins. The sheriff returned with the gun, the family car, a 1940 Buick, and Robert Huggins, who was taken into custody for investigation. The following day, Robert Huggins and the Buick were released; the target pistol and the

Cecile Huggins

two slugs retrieved from Ben Sain's body and from the wrecked automobile were sent to the Bureau of Criminal Investigation for testing.

Then, on Friday afternoon, Cecile Huggins was brought by the sheriff's deputies to the Common Pleas Courtroom on the third floor of the impressive Greco-Roman courthouse just across the street from the jail. His attorneys, Enyeart and Dixon, and his family were gathered in the courtroom. Justice of the Peace Leo Gross occupied the judge's chair just behind the massive, hand-carved walnut bar. Court reporter Helen Foley sat poised at her desk directly in front of the bar, three freshly sharpened pencils and a steno pad close at hand. Prosecuting Attorney Jim DeWeese was the last to arrive—and the first to speak. "If it please the Court, the State moves for a continuance of the preliminary hearing in this matter for a reasonable period of time. As counsel for the Defendant is aware, we have located a gun, but it has been sent to the BCI for testing and we do not yet have the results of those tests. By the same token, we do not have the gun available to us today. Moreover the county coroner is presently out of town. For those reasons, the State is unable to proceed this afternoon."

Harley Enyeart, crusty and feisty as was his wont, nearly fell over his crutches in his rush to get to his feet to express his strident objection to the prosecutor's motion. He had been cruelly crippled from a bout with polio at age two, but disdained the use of a wheelchair and insisted on making do with no more than a pair of crutches. He also lived with constant and severe back pain, all of which may have contributed to his abrasive, caustic manner. "Objection, Your Honor!" he fairly snarled. "If the State has any kind of case at all, they should be ready to proceed now—as scheduled. Our client has already been detained without bail for more than a week. If the State is unable to go forward, the Defendant should be discharged. That's the law."

Jim DeWeese remained on his feet until Enyeart had finished his tirade.

Harley D. Enyeart

Then, while Enyeart struggled back into his chair and fumed, DeWeese calmly responded, "Your Honor, a postponement of the preliminary hearing will be for the protection of the Defendant, as well as a benefit to the State because it will afford both parties more time for proper investigation and preparation. As everyone here is aware, I just returned from vacation and have been fully occupied with my preparations for the Grand Jury, which meets next week. And, as Mr. Enyeart properly points out, there is indeed a law that applies. The statute in question provides that the Defendant is entitled to a preliminary hearing *within 10 days* after a plea has been entered. It *also* provides that a postponement may nonetheless be granted for good cause shown. We respectfully submit that the unavailability of the gun and the results of the ballistic test—*and* the absence of the coroner— constitute good cause."

Bill Dixon, Enyeart's younger and calmer law partner placed his hand on Enyeart's shoulder, and rose to address the Justice. "We would agree, Your Honor, that the statute is as represented by Mr. DeWeese," he conceded. "And for that reason, we are prepared to agree to a postponement until Thursday of next week."

Jim DeWeese suggested the hearing be postponed only until the following Wednesday at 1:00 p.m. and all parties—including the curmudgeonly Enyeart—agreed.

As it happened, the wily DeWeese had an ace up his sleeve. When the grand jury convened in secret session the following Monday, he presented the case to that body "on his own information" and presented his evidence, including testimony from Emery Galloway, a ballistics expert from the BCI, and the results of his testing of the gun recovered from the Huggins household. When the grand jury, through its foreman, Joseph Thoma, made its anticipated report to Judge Porter on Wednesday morning, it included 35 indictments, the most notable of which was an indictment against Cecile Huggins for the first-degree murder of Ben Sain.

Harley Enyeart was absolutely infuriated when he learned that he had been end-played by the prosecutor. He spent the noon hour in his office library looking through volume after volume for relevant legal authority with which to challenge the indictment, but found little support. Then, at one o'clock that afternoon, when all the parties convened for the scheduled preliminary hearing, Jim DeWeese rose and addressed his remarks to Justice Gross, "Your Honor, inasmuch as the Grand Jury has already returned an indictment against this Defendant, the State has no desire to proceed with, or even to attend, the preliminary hearing scheduled for this afternoon."

An irate Harley Enyeart once again struggled to his feet and, supported by the counsel table, glowered, first at DeWeese, then at Justice Gross, "Your Honor, this is preposterous! The law provides that the Defendant is entitled to a preliminary hearing and we all agreed that the same should be held today—at one o'clock. We insist on the Defendant's right to that hearing." And as if his demeanor and his strident tone had not been sufficient to convey the full measure of his ire, he appended an acerbic, "And I mean *now. Right now*—as scheduled by order of this Court."

To which DeWeese blithely responded, "The State has no objection to the Court's proceeding with the scheduled preliminary hearing. By all means, have at it. We simply recognize that since the Defendant has already been indicted, the preliminary hearing has been rendered entirely superfluous and we have no wish to participate in a meaningless charade."

And, of course, he was right. Without the State's participation, and the presentation of its evidence, there was nothing to refute. The scheduled preliminary hearing was simply cancelled—much to Enyeart's consternation.

Five days later, on October 8, Cecile Huggins, dressed in gray slacks and a red sweater, and flanked by his two attorneys, appeared in Judge Porter's courtroom and stood while Clerk of Courts Earl Mishler read the indictment charging him with first degree murder. Because the law required that he enter the plea on his own behalf, rather than by counsel, he personally addressed the Court and mildly entered his plea of "Not Guilty."

Judge Porter accepted the plea and set the matter for trial beginning Monday, November 26.

3

Notwithstanding the Trial Court's order scheduling Cecile Huggins' trial for November 26, that was simply not to be. On November 8, a superceding order was docketed. That order is wholly self-explanatory and reads as follows:

> *William M. Dixon, one of the attorneys for the within defendant appeared in open court this 6th day of November, 1951 and suggested to the court that the defendant is not now sane, and presented to the court a certificate of Dr. E. R. Torrence to that effect, and upon consideration thereof the court orders that this matter be continued for hearing upon the question of the present sanity or insanity of the defendant, and the defendant is ordered to be committed to the Lima State Hospital where he shall remain under observation for a period of not more than one month and after a careful examination of said defendant said institution shall report in writing to this court its finding as to the mental condition of the defendant at the time of the examination, together with such recommendations, suggestions and opinions as may be helpful to the court, which report shall also contain the names and addresses of the parties making the examination.*
>
> *It is further ordered that the defendant be remanded to the custody of the sheriff and that the proper papers be issued by the clerk to the sheriff of this county for the transporting of the defendant to said institution.*
>
> *David S. Porter, Judge*

It has long been the law of Ohio that the mere suggestion that a criminal defendant might not be sufficiently sane to aid and consult with his counsel, and to stand trial for the offense charged, mandates that he be referred for examination and evaluation concerning his present sanity—not his sanity at the time of the offense, but his sanity as of the time of trial. In 1951, such referrals were routinely made to the Lima State Hospital for the Criminally Insane. Jim DeWeese objected only to the introduction of Dr. Torrence's letter, as well as documents from Huggins' military records. "These documents have no place in the record at this juncture," he said. "The only thing required is counsel's suggestion that the Defendant may not be presently sane; nothing further is needed. The State has no objection to the mandated evaluation."

Despite the Prosecutor's concession, Dixon insisted on advising the Court that Huggins had been in a stupor for the past few days, could not communicate with his counsel, and had been examined by Dr. Clarence Hackett of the local Guidance Center who had found Huggins to be "...suffering from a catatonic stupor, a species of schizophrenia or dementia praecox." Again DeWeese advised the Court that the State was perfectly agreeable to the referral and would expect a full hearing on the issue of Huggins' present sanity when he is returned from Lima State.

"What do you think they're up to?" asked Assistant Prosecutor J. Richard Gaier after the hearing.

"Nothing that I hadn't expected," answered DeWeese. "In cases where the evidence against the defendant is as strong as it is here, it's almost routine. They're laying the groundwork for an insanity defense; it's really all they've got. They can't really argue that Huggins didn't kill Ben Sain; they can only argue that he didn't understand the nature and quality of his act, or if he did, he couldn't help himself."

"What! 'Irresistible impulse?' What a load of crap! You're not buyin' into that bullshit, are you?" queried Gaier, a short, thickly set man in his late twenties with an aggressive, feisty manner.

"Don't know yet. We'll see what the Lima State shrinks say." DeWeese awaited Gaier's reaction; then when none came, he added, "Who knows? He may really be insane."

"Seems to me this catatonic stupor is mighty convenient," argued Gaier. "Sounds like pure bullshit to me. Stupor would be pretty easy to fake."

"Tell me about it," said DeWeese sarcastically. "But it does sound like he may have some history to support an argument. We'll see what Lima says."

4

And, in accordance with Judge Porter's order, Cecile Huggins was returned from Lima within the prescribed one-month period. With him came a letter report from Dr. E. R. Bushong, the Lima State Superintendent, which recited, in part, that:

> *This is with reference to the above-named colored man who was committed to this hospital from your court on November 8, 1951, for thirty days' mental observation under the provisions of Section 13441-4 G. C.*
>
> *It is obvious that there is definitely something wrong with Huggins, and our findings coincide to a great extent with those revealed by the Veterans Administration. It appears that he was given several mental examinations between 1945 and 1949, and each time he was found to be psychotic in varying degrees of severity. As we see him at present, he is mildly stuporous, shows much mental blocking, is isolated, withdrawn and abnormally quiet. There is a bizarre element shown in his remarks along with more or less suspicion. He impresses us as having been very acutely psychotic at one time and has never fully recovered.*
>
> *It is our opinion that Huggins is legally insane and irresponsible. We are ready to turn him over to your officers.*

In point of fact, Dr. Bushong actually answered the wrong question. Huggins' commitment by the Court was for the purpose of ascertaining whether he was *presently sufficiently sane to consult with his counsel and to stand trial*—

not whether he was "legally responsible" at the time of his having killed Ben Sain. Nonetheless, the answer was accepted as evidence of his inability to stand trial and Judge Porter promptly scheduled a hearing on that single issue for December 26.

The hearing itself lasted less than one day. The Defense had the burden of proof and was amply supported by the testimony of Dr. Bushong, who testified in accordance with his letter report—and upon cross-examination by DeWeese—ultimately responded to the correct question, and expressed his opinion Huggins was not, at that time, sane enough to consult with counsel and to participate meaningfully in a trial to determine his guilt or innocence of the offense charged.

Dr. Bushong's testimony was buttressed by that of Drs. Torrence and Hackett, as well as that of nine lay witnesses, members of Huggins' family and friends. Jim DeWeese presented no evidence on behalf of the State. In view of the opinion rendered by the Lima State Hospital Superintendent, there was nothing he could do to change the outcome. Judge Porter had no choice other than to commit Huggins "to the care and custody of the Lima State Hospital until he be restored to reason, and upon being restored to reason, he shall be proceeded against as provided by law."

"You need to remember," DeWeese chided a greatly disgruntled Dick Gaier, "that the Judge had no alternative. The law says that if Lima State finds him to be insane, the Judge has to recommit him. You also need to remember that he hasn't been found to be not guilty by reason of insanity; this only means that he's incompetent to stand trial. And he'll be held in a cell until Lima says he's sufficiently sane to be tried. Then, when that happens, the real question will be whether he was sane at the time he put a bullet in Ben Sain's head. That question is still open—and it'll remain open and Huggins will remain in custody until Lima says he's sufficiently sane to stand trial—if ever."

5

Cecile Huggins spent the next 3,575 days, nearly eight years, cooped up in a one-room cell at Lima State Hospital before he was returned to Miami County for trial. Precisely how he passed those days is not completely known. That which is known is that he was regularly examined, evaluated and medicated by the Lima State team of psychiatrists and psychologists, and that he spent most of his free time in a stuporous state, either real or feigned, all the while sitting virtually motionless on his cot or on the floor of his cell, quietly and unobtrusively contemplating his bleak surroundings, his toes, his knees and his navel.

During that 3,575 days, Harry S. Truman completed the last full year of his Presidency; a long and arduous battle for America's top job ensued, and Dwight D. Eisenhower, served one full term and nearly three years of a second term as President; the Korean War ended; Julius and Ethel Rosenberg were sentenced and executed for treason; Ford Motor Company's innovative Edsel motor car flopped miserably at a cost of millions; Ben Hogan captured his fourth and last U.S. Open title; the New York Yankees and the Brooklyn Dodgers dominated the World Series, winning four and two of the eight series played during that time, and the World Heavyweight Boxing title was passed from Jersey Joe Walcott to Rocky Marciano to Floyd Patterson to Ingemar Johansson. Perhaps of more local interest, the Ohio State football team, under Woody Hayes and led by Hopalong Cassidy, won the 1954 National Championship.

And all the while, Cecile Huggins still appeared to be absorbed by his toes, knees and navel. Then, finally—and perhaps inexplicably—the Allen County Court of Appeals, on the basis of testimony from Lima State's Dr. Theodore Reshetylo, determined that Huggins was sufficiently restored to sanity as to permit him to consult with counsel and stand trial for the murder of Ben Sain, and the hospital authorities were accordingly ordered to return him to Miami County for that purpose. That order was obtained with the assistance of Attorney Joe DaPore of Lima, who would remain in the murder case as Harley Enyeart's new co-counsel, primarily because Bill Dixon had, during Cecile's 3,575 days, become Troy's Law Director and was thereby disqualified to continue as one of Huggins' defense counsel.

The first order of business upon Huggins' return to Miami County was to arraign him on the still-pending murder indictment. That event occurred on October 27, 1959, when he appeared again in Judge Porter's courtroom, flanked by both Enyeart and DaPore, and entered the double plea of 'Not Guilty' and 'Not Guilty by Reason of Insanity.' Judge Porter accepted the two pleas, set the case for trial to a jury beginning Monday, November 30, 1959, at 9:30 a.m., and directed Clerk of Courts Earl Mishler to cause the Jury Commissioners to draw a special venire of seventy-five jurors for that purpose in the manner provided by law.

The special venire was drawn that same day and the current Sheriff, Robert Henning, was ordered to cause each of the seventy-five prospective jurors whose names had been drawn from the jury wheel to be summoned into court on November 30. That procedure, too, was promptly accomplished and Sheriff Henning reported on November 3 that all seventy-five members of the special venire had been properly summoned.

As it happened, however, none of the veniremen had to appear for the trial. In mid-November, less than two weeks before the scheduled trial, Harley Enyeart and Joe DaPore paid a surprise visit to Jim DeWeese's office. "Got a proposition for you, Jim," said the experienced, urbane DaPore, "one you can't refuse."

"Have you now?" queried DeWeese. "Let me guess. You guys are prepared to plead Huggins out if I'll take the death penalty off the table, right?"

Harley Enyeart made a rude snort. "Not hardly, Jim. Not even close. You know both of us better than that."

"Somehow, Harley," DeWeese laughed easily, "I hadn't really expected you to throw in the towel quite yet. What've you got in mind?"

Joe DaPore took over for his irascible co-counsel. It was a good choice; he was known to be the more reasonable, conciliatory member of the new defense team. "Try this one out, Jim," he said. "I think it makes sense for all of us. You reduce the charge to manslaughter, and we'll have the Defendant waive his right to a jury and opt to be tried by a three-judge court. And," he continued, "we won't plead 'not guilty' to the manslaughter charge; we'll only plead the insanity defense. We'll agree not to contest the issue whether or not he killed Sain. We won't admit it, but we won't deny it either."

"Now explain to me," demanded DeWeese, "just why in hell I should agree to that?"

DaPore was totally unruffled by DeWeese's explosive response. "Let me try to do just that, okay?"

"I'm listening," said DeWeese skeptically.

"That's all we ask, Jim," DaPore replied congenially. "Look at it this way. As matters now stand, you've got to prove that Huggins deliberately and with pre-meditated malice killed Ben Sain. I acknowledge that you can probably still do it—but remember, it's been more than eight years since Sain was killed and you've probably lost some valuable witnesses over that period of time. It will doubtless be more difficult to prove all the elements today than it would have been eight years ago, and if you can't prove your case, Huggins goes free. The State will have no further control over him and we don't have to prove he was ever insane—whether he was or not. That becomes a non-issue."

"And?" queried DeWeese.

"And, if we don't deny his guilt—but don't actually admit it either—all you have to do is make a *prima facie* showing and you'll get a conviction for manslaughter. Unless, of course, his insanity defense flies, in which case, he gets acquitted, but in that case he gets recommitted to Lima State. Either way, he's still in custody—either pursuant to a manslaughter conviction or on a finding of insanity. And," he added, "the only issue the Court will have to decide is whether or not he was sane when he killed Sain. Little play on words there, but it is what it is."

DeWeese frowned, "I'd rather have him for murder one and put him away for life..."

"I understand that," conceded DaPore, "but if you do not get him for murder, he walks; I can't imagine you would want that to happen."

"True enough," admitted DeWeese. "I sure as hell don't want him walking the streets again." He scratched at his chin and added, "But we both know that Lima's probably going to find him to be presently sane and release him again."

"But at least you'll have some control over him," coaxed DaPore.

"I don't like it much," grumbled DeWeese. "But it does make some kind of sense. Let me think about it awhile. I'll get back to you."

Then, just a few days later, on November 23, Jim DeWeese amended the indictment in such a manner as to reduce the charge against Huggins from first-degree murder to simple manslaughter, and Huggins entered a plea on the reduced charge of "Not guilty by reason of insanity." He also waived his right to trial by jury and elected to be tried by a panel of three judges. Upon that state of affairs, Judge Porter, as presiding judge, selected Judge John Kiracofe of Preble County and Judge Huber Beery of Shelby County to hear the case with him. The trial would begin on December 2, as scheduled.

6

A trial to the Court—be it one judge or three—without the intervention of a jury can be thoroughly and efficiently conducted far more expeditiously than a trial to a jury. Time-consuming side-bar conferences, legal arguments on motions and proffers of evidence, out of the hearing of the jury, become unnecessary; the rules of evidence can be relaxed somewhat; the Court can take "judicial notice" of matters which would otherwise have to be proven to a jury; and the oft-times difficult logistics of convening, reconvening and otherwise accommodating the needs and exigencies of 12 separate and essentially uninitiated laymen can all be dispensed with if there is no jury to be considered. And for that reason—and because the issue as to whether Ben Sain had actually died at the hands of Cecile Huggins had been essentially eliminated from the case—the trial proceeded in a brisk, workmanlike manner.

Because of the necessity of making his *prima facie* showing that Huggins had fired the fatal shot into Ben Sain's head and thereby caused his death, Jim DeWeese began his evidence with the testimony of Darrell Taylor, of Lima, Ohio, who told the judges that he had witnessed the altercation between Huggins and Sain at the corner of Main and Elm Streets in Troy on the evening of September 20, 1951 and that their argument had soon degenerated into a physical fight; he also told the judges that after the fight had been broken up, Huggins had gone home, gotten an automobile and chased Sain up the North Dixie highway. Taylor also said he had known that Huggins had access to a handgun and had actually seen one in his hand directly after the killing.

Although Coroner William Adkins had been subpoenaed for the Prosecution, he was unavailable and, to simplify matters, the parties stipulated that if present, he would have testified that Sain's death was caused by a .22 caliber bullet which he had personally extracted from the man's brain.

The next prosecution witness was Emery Galloway from the BCI, who testified that the bullet taken from Sain's brain had been fired from the .22 caliber target pistol found under the bottom drawer of a dresser in Huggins' room. He was followed by former Sheriff Dick Seifried, who testified that Huggins had admitted that he had fought with Sain that evening, but denied any knowledge of the shooting. Former Chief Deputy Robert Henning, who had succeeded Seifried as sheriff, told the Court of his having found seven live cartridges and two bullet casings in the gun recovered from Huggins' home.

Then, having made his *prima facie* case against the Defendant, the Prosecution rested its case before the end of the first day of trial.

Prior to the presentation of the Defendant's evidence, DaPore and Enyeart formally advised the Court that the Defendant neither admitted nor denied that he had caused Sain's death. The sole issue in the case, they and the Prosecution agreed, was whether or not their client was responsible for what he had done in 1951 because he was mentally unbalanced—legally insane—at the time.

The following morning DaPore and Enyeart opened their client's defense with testimony from Lima State's Dr. Reshetylo, who testified that "taking into consideration previous findings in Huggins' medical history, he was more than probably mentally ill" when the crime was committed, and that he "more than probably could not distinguish right from wrong at that time." Dr. Henry Luidens, Lima State's hospital superintendent, simply corroborated and reiterated Dr. Reshetylo's opinions. Both of the Lima State psychiatrists based their opinions on the Defendant's military and Veterans' Administration records, and DaPore offered those medical records into evidence as Defense exhibits.

Jim DeWeese's cross-examination of the two Lima State doctors was scarcely perfunctory in nature; it might even be fair to say that he went after them with hammer and tongs. He began his assault with a thorough critique of their professional credentials, their medical education, experience—and their licensure. That particular line of attack requires some explanation. In the aftermath of World War II, many of the refugees from war-ravaged Europe were reputable, talented and properly licensed to practice their professions within the nations from which they had been forced to escape to America; however, the laws of the individual states in this country required that they be examined and become licensed by the state within which they intended to practice in order to engage in their respective professional specialties—and that was often a virtually insurmountable process for those displaced professionals. For that reason, most of the psychiatrists who had immigrated to this country ultimately found it necessary to exercise their professional expertise in the service of state-controlled institutions rather than in private practice.

"Doctor," demanded DeWeese of each of the Lima State doctors, "are you licensed to practice psychiatry by the State of Ohio?" Or, in the alternative, "I understand that you are entitled to the title and emoluments of 'Doctor', but isn't it a fact that you are disqualified by law from the practice of medicine—or, more specifically, psychiatry—in this jurisdiction?"

His examination of each of the doctors would then proceed to questions as to the number and nature of the respective examinations, evaluations and observations they had made of the Defendant during his confinement at Lima State Hospital. "Describe, if you will, what tests were administered." "What was the purpose of each of these tests?" "What did you learn from each of these tests?" "Is that recorded on the patient's chart?" "Please show the Court the entry you made on the patient's chart after each of the tests, examinations and evaluations you have described?" "What treatments were administered?" and "Were all of the procedures performed in accordance with approved medical standards?" And so on, virtually *ad nauseum.*

DeWeese's questioning took other tacks as well. One of his target areas was the doctors' reliance on Huggins' military and Veterans' Administration medical evaluations. "Doctor, have you come into this Court to express your own opinions or to simply regurgitate that which you understood from your reading of these 15-year-old documents that you somehow acquired from various government agencies?" "May we expect the persons who prepared those reports to appear in this case so that we can question them concerning what they wrote about Mr. Huggins 15 years ago?" "No?" he demanded. "Do we even know who the persons are who created these records upon which you have relied? Or what their own qualifications are? Or, I should ask, what their qualifications were 15 years ago?" And so on in that vein as well.

And finally, as a part of his cross-examination of each of the doctors, he got to the real issue. "Doctor, you have testified as to your opinion of the Defendant's mental condition during the time he was under your care at Lima State Hospital over the last eight years or so, and you have expressed your opinion that he was legally insane during most of that time, is that correct?"

To which question each of the doctors answered affirmatively.

"But, you would agree that you did not find him to be consistently insane during that entire time, would you not?"

"No sir, I would not agree with that. He has been consistently insane during that entire time."

"Did you not tell the Allen County Court of Appeals, just within the last three months, that Mr. Huggins was sufficiently recovered to participate in this proceeding? To assist and consult with his counsel and to otherwise participate in this trial?"

"Well, yes, but that was only recently."

"You mean that as of a few months ago, he was sane?"

"Yes."

"Then let me ask you again whether you found Mr. Huggins to be consistently insane during the entire time of his confinement at Lima State?"

The witness fidgeted and shifted his position on the stand. "Perhaps I misunderstood your question. Certainly a patient can improve—or regress—either while under treatment or, on occasion, spontaneously."

"You do understand," asked DeWeese, "that the issue in this case is not whether Mr. Huggins was insane while under your care, observation and treatment at Lima State Hospital, do you not?"

"Yes, sir."

"And that the real issue is whether he was legally insane on September 20, 1951; do you understand that?"

"Yes sir, but we didn't see him on that date."

"Precisely," snapped DeWeese. "You didn't see him on September 20, 1951, and for that reason you are certainly not qualified to express an opinion concerning his mental condition on that date. Is that fair?"

'Well, of course, he may have been in a state of remission on that particular day—and that may be true as of today. But we do know that he has had a history of mental illness dating back to the early 1940s and was deemed to be 'not responsible' for whatever anti-social activities he may have committed."

"Which were?" queried DeWeese.

"We don't actually know the details; the records were not clear as to what those acts might have been. However, we do know that after eight and a half months of service, he received an honorable discharge from the U. S. Navy and was awarded a 30 percent disability for a 'psychotic' condition. The records also indicate that he was examined and hospitalized on several occasions following his discharge, each time with a finding that his earlier mental illness had not disappeared completely."

DeWeese repeated the latter part of the answer. "'...that his earlier mental illness had not disappeared completely.' Is that what you just said?"

"Yes sir."

"May I presume, then, that the records on which your present opinion is based show that his mental illness was not consistently persistent?"

"Well, yes, sir. If you put it that way, we'd have to concede that to be the case. In the grand scheme of things, there are variations in the levels of mental illness. Some days, weeks or even months, his condition may be better or worse than others. That's really the nature of mental illness."

"In view of that answer, Doctor, how is it that you can come into Court today, more than 8 years after the event—not having seen or examined Cecile Huggins until sometime in mid-November of 1951—and tell this Court that he was legally insane and not responsible for his actions on September 20 of that year."

"Well, sir. As you intimate, it would be impossible for us to positively 'certify' the precise level of his illness on that specific date. However, based on the history we have looked at, and our own examinations over the past eight years, we can most certainly conclude that he was probably insane on the specific date you mention."

"Probably insane?" demanded Deweese. "Is that the best you can do? That he was probably insane?"

"Yes, sir. That sums it up pretty well."

"In the final analysis, then, you're guessing. Is that correct?"

"It's certainly an educated guess. Not having seen him on that specific day, it is the best we can do. It nonetheless remains our concerted opinion that he was probably insane and not legally responsible when he took the life of his victim."

"Doctor, is it possible that his 'mental illness' was at a low level—virtually undetectable—at the time he killed Mr. Sain, and that the subsequent realization of the enormity of his act, the deliberate taking of a human life, triggered a major relapse in his condition?"

"Anything is possible, sir."

The Messrs. DaPore and Enyeart called, as their third and final witness, Dr. R. A. Thomas, of Piqua, Ohio. Dr. Thomas was a staff psychiatrist at the Upper Valley Guidance Center. He told the Court that he had first examined Huggins just a few months ago, and based his testimony on "symptomatic findings, which must have existed for many years." His opinion was expressed in a slightly different manner from those expressed by the Lima State doctors. The principal thrust of his testimony was that the Defendant probably could not have distinguished right from wrong on September 20, 1951.

Jim DeWeese's cross-examination of Dr. Thomas was substantially similar to that to which he had subjected the Lima State doctors over a period of the past two days. When that ordeal had worn itself down,

Judge Porter announced that the military and Veterans' Administration records, proffered earlier by defense counsel, would be admitted over the Prosecution's vehement objections. It was improper, DeWeese argued, for the Court to consider records prepared by persons not available for cross-examination—or for the Court to consider the testimony of the Lima State Psychiatrists to the extent that it was predicated upon those same records. It was, he insisted, a clear violation of the so-called hearsay rule of evidence.

Despite DeWeese's fervent resistance, the records were admitted into evidence—and the Defense rested its case.

Jim DeWeese's rebuttal evidence was presented Friday morning and was mercifully brief. He simply re-called Sheriff Henning and former Sheriff Richard Seifried and asked them to describe Huggins' attitude and demeanor at the time of his arrest and during the early days of his confinement in the county jail. It was only after he had been in custody for some two weeks' time, they agreed, that his 'stuporous behavior' began to manifest itself. They were both satisfied that it was either feigned or triggered by the event itself.

And the Prosecution rested its case in rebuttal. The trial was over; all that remained was for the three-judge panel to consider the evidence and to announce its decision.

Two days later, on Saturday afternoon, December 14, the Court announced its unanimous decision; they had found Huggins to be not guilty by reason of insanity. The formal order of acquittal was entered the following Monday and contained an order that Huggins be remanded and committed to Lima State Hospital "until such time as he may be released in accordance with law."

"Well, you called one thing right," mused a sorely dismayed Dick Gaier after he had reviewed and digested the Court's finding of 'not guilty by reason of insanity' and its order of re-commitment of Huggins to Lima State.

"How's that?" asked a sour, but nonetheless somewhat bemused DeWeese.

"I seem to remember your having conceded that if the Court were to acquit Huggins of the manslaughter charge, the State would still have some measure of control over him—and, of course, that's exactly what's happened," said Gaier. "Even though he's been cleared of the criminal charge, we've still got him in custody. So, I guess you got it right after all."

"Don't kid yourself, Dick," responded DeWeese. "He'll be back on the streets in less than thirty days."

"What makes you think so?" inquired Gaier.

"I've been down this road before and I know very well that before the week is out Joe DaPore will apply for his release and the Lima shrinks will have no choice other than to find him fit to be released; they're already on record that he was competent to stand trial. They're virtually estopped from finding him 'unfit to be released'—or if they don't release him on their own initiative, you can bet that the Court of Appeals for Allen County will let him out on a writ of *habeas corpus*—based on the shrinks' testimony and their 'clinical findings.'"

"It's not quite the same question," argued Gaier. "It's one thing that they've said he was sane enough to stand trial; it's quite another to find that he's been completely restored to sanity and is therefore fit to be released."

"You're exactly right," conceded DeWeese. "It's 'apples and oranges'—and they know it as well as we do. But you can bet they'll release him as essentially cured."

"Then..."

"Wanna bet on it?" asked DeWeese.

"No bets," answered Gaier. "You've been through it before. But why..."

"Why did I agree to the deal?"

"Right. What did we gain by reducing the charge?"

"Think about it, Dick," answered DeWeese. "Whether we tried him for murder or for manslaughter, we were gonna have to fight the insanity defense—and the result would have been the same either way. If we'd had the burden of proving all the elements of first-degree murder, a jury just might have found that we hadn't met the burden and he walks away clean. This way, he's not denied that he killed Ben Sain and that's on his record; we've established that he's capable of killing—and may well commit other acts of violence in future—and if he does, they'll have to put him away for life. In fact, I should imagine that a simple assault—in the future—would be sufficient justification for a long-term commitment.

"So, in the final analysis, we will have some small measure of control over him. Not as much as I'd have liked, but it's better than none."

7

Jim DeWeese did have it right. Cecile Huggins was promptly released from Lima State Hospital on the basis of the psychiatrists' assurances that he was no longer sufficiently mentally ill to justify his further confinement. He returned to his family in Troy and never again found meaningful or suitable employment—partly because of his history, and partly because of his disinclination to perform work of any sort. His brother Robert was successful in soliciting a job for him with a local masonry contractor, but Cecile declined the offer. He continued in residence at his parents' home and subsisted on his disability compensation from the Veterans' Administration.

He was, ever after, considered by all who knew of him to be more than a little eccentric and potentially dangerous. He spent his time wandering about the town, either on foot or on his bicycle, clad, both summer and winter, in a long, heavy, woolen coat that nearly swept the ground and an over-sized, floppy hat that nearly touched his shoulders, all the while either singing aloud or playing his ever-present harmonica. And while many who knew his history were careful not to offend him or to otherwise incur his wrath, he was never again known to have committed any act of violence or to have had any serious trouble with the law.

There were rumors, of course, but nothing of any consequence was ever proven. He never married and died in a Columbus nursing home in April of 2004, at the age of seventy-seven.

AUTHOR'S NOTE

I had known Cecile Huggins from the time I began grade school at the old Edwards School on West Main Street. He was some two years older than I, but his younger brother Robert—Bobby—was my own age and a good friend of mine. In fact, I met him on my first day of school when we were both just six years old. And, I'm embarrassed to admit that I hadn't known any of the "colored" community at that time and, for that reason, was unable to resist bringing him home with me to show him to my mother. She fed us both milk and cookies and we spent the afternoon playing with my meager collection of tin soldiers, marbles, and Indian arrowheads harvested from my grandfather's farm by the Stillwater River. We remained good friends through grade school and, because we were of approximately equal size, we were frequently matched as boxing opponents during physical education classes. And while neither of us pulled any punches, I am happy to report that we were careful not to really hurt each other either. He went on to earn a number of Golden Gloves championships and I was only too happy that our sparring days ended at about the same time. I was no longer a match for him.

It was through Bobby that I came to know—and to like—his older brother Cecile, but I never really knew him well. I do remember that one of the high points of my young life occurred when he asked me to be a member of a six-man football team he was assembling to meet and defeat all comers. As it happened, we never had a practice or played a game, but I was nonetheless a very proud young fifth-grader.

I was out of town, newly married and in my second year of law school when Cecile shot and killed Ben Sain, but I was deeply affected and followed the case closely. I was greatly surprised, both by his actions and by the suggestion that he might have been mentally ill. I had never been aware that either his behavior or his psyche was anything other than perfectly normal, and for many years I had believed that he must have feigned mental illness in order to beat the system. Now, having made a study of his travails through the courts and the psychiatric wards, I am inclined to agree that the doctors' judgments in that regard were probably correct.

POSTSCRIPT

I don't know that I can leave the subject of the law's treatment of criminal defendants thought to be mentally ill without sharing an anecdote from my own professional experience.

In the mid-1960s I found myself in the position of defense counsel for an elderly farmer who had been indicted for multiple forgery offenses. On the occasion set for his preliminary hearing, it was suggested by Jim DeWeese's Chief Assistant Prosecutor, Robert Huffman, that my client might be mentally ill, and based on that suggestion, Judge Porter had no alternative other than to send him off to Lima State for evaluation.

To tell the truth, I had also considered my client to be somewhat unbalanced and therefore had no argument with Huffman's suggestion. The basis for my own opinion in that regard lay in the fact that every time I met with him to discuss his case, he was more interested in regaling me with stories about his pet horse, which he claimed rode about with him in the back seat of his passenger automobile when he came to town to carry out his errands, than he was in discussing the defense of his pending criminal case.

He lived alone, he told me, and was concerned about finding someone to care for his pet horse—and to drive him about—if he had to go to jail on the multiple forgery charges. And, try as I might, I couldn't induce him to forget about the damned horse and to help me keep him out of jail.

I think he sensed that I didn't believe his stories about his pet horse because he challenged me to visit his farm and see for myself that such an animal actually existed. In any event, because of his somewhat bizarre behavior and because of his insistence that "Harold" was actually a real horse and enjoyed riding with him in his automobile, I was certainly dubious about his mental stability and therefore had no objection to his referral to Lima State for examination. And, of course, some thirty days later the report from Lima, finding my client to be hopelessly insane and grossly delusional, came back with a recommendation that he be committed to their care "indefinitely" which, of course, had the potential to be a life sentence. That recommendation, if accepted by the Court, would be far more disastrous for my client than the slap on the wrist he could expect if convicted on the first-offense forgery charges, and I therefore felt it necessary to challenge Lima State's report and their recommendation.

The case was scheduled for a one-day trial on the sole issue of my client's competence to stand trial. By way of preparation, I had thoroughly reviewed and critiqued the Lima State report, which just coincidentally had been authored by the same Dr. Reshetylo who had testified concerning Cecile Huggins' mental condition. By the same token, I was unable to find an expert who was willing to confirm my client's competence, so it developed that my entire case would necessarily depend on whatever damage I could inflict on Dr. Reshetylo's opinions on cross-examination.

The evening before trial just happened to be my regular golf and poker night at the country club, but my upcoming trial was nonetheless not far from my thoughts. Along about ten o'clock, I had an unexpected brain hiccough and temporarily relinquished my seat at the poker table to an onlooker. I then enlisted Bobby Ploughar, the club bartender, to take a ride with me; we'd be back, I assured him, in less than an hour.

Actually, we were back in forty minutes, and I resumed my seat at the table and won the grand sum of three dollars by the time the game broke up. Before leaving the club I asked Bobby to be available the next afternoon.

The competency hearing began the following morning at nine o'clock and, as anticipated, Bob Huffman's entire case on the issue of my client's alleged mental illness consisted of the testimony of Dr. Reshetylo, who testified in precise accordance with his official report. He told the jury of his interviews with my client and described the varied esoteric tests he had administered, and upon the basis of the test results and his several examinations, he expressed the conclusion that the Defendant was, indeed, hopelessly insane.

My cross-examination of Dr. Reshetylo proceeded pretty much along the same lines as those utilized by Jim DeWeese in the Huggins trial, i.e.

we discussed the witness's credentials, qualifications and experience; the significance of his various test results; the bases for his expressed opinions, etc. Then, finally, I told him, "Thank you, Doctor, I think that's all the questions I have."

And, just as he began to step down from the witness stand, I stopped him. "I'm sorry, Doctor, but I have just one more question."

He resumed his seat with an air of expectancy. "All right, sir. Not a problem."

"Did the Defendant happen to mention to you that he had a horse named Harold that rode with him in the back seat of his automobile?"

At which, Dr. Reshetylo actually laughed, "Yes sir, he most certainly did."

"Did you believe him?"

"No, no, of course not," he answered.

"Did he insist on it?"

"Yes, he did. I couldn't convince him just how ridiculous that sounded."

"Did that insistence play any part in the formation of the opinions you've expressed here today?"

"Of course it did. Actually, that's probably the primary basis for my opinion. He was clearly delusional and would brook no argument on the subject."

"Thank you, Doctor. I think that's all."

I did call one witness to the stand that afternoon. I called Bobby Ploughar. In response to my questions, he identified himself and his occupation.

"Did you see me last night?" I asked.

Bobby broke into a wide grin as he answered, "I sure did."

"Did we take a short trip together?"

"Yes sir."

"Tell the jury where we went and what we did."

"Well, sir, it was about 10:30 and you drove me to a farm down on Route 40, near Englewood, and led me around to the barn. It looked like there wasn't anybody home and you removed one of the windows from the dark side of the barn. You said you had the owner's permission—and we both went in through the window."

"Please tell the jury what, if anything, you saw in the barn."

"Uh, you'd brought along a flashlight and shined it around the inside of the barn, and I saw a coupla cows, some chickens and a goat..."

"Anything else?" I prompted.

"Oh yeah," he said. "There was this *wee little horse*—his head was no higher than my belt line," he said as he stood from the witness stand and indicated his belt line.

And the jury broke up with laughter. Twenty minutes later, they found my client to be perfectly sane.

Then, after the jury had been thanked for their service and dismissed, I approached the bench and announced to the Court that my client's plea to the forgery charge was "not guilty" and "not guilty by reason of insanity."

Bob Huffman, who, just incidentally, was a fine attorney and a good friend of mine, was visibly taken aback. "You can't do that! This jury just found him to be fully completely sane."

"Actually, Bob," I countered. "I can—and I just did. That issue will be tried to a different jury, and your Dr. Reshetylo will be my best witness."

"He's right," Judge Porter agreed. "I've already recorded the dual pleas. You'll both want to prepare for trial."

And, as it happened, we didn't need to try the matter. Huffman ultimately dismissed all but one of the forgery charges and my client pled guilty to that one. He was ordered to make restitution on all the forged checks as a condition of his two-year probation and was released from custody.

KISSES

1

It could not be said of Marguerite Carmean that she was one of those fortunate young people whom we are oft-times inclined to characterize as being "lucky in love." Through no apparent fault of her own, she seemed to possess an uncanny knack for picking losers.

Born in Noblesville, Indiana, in 1909, she and her siblings, a brother and a sister, were raised and educated in that city until their parents, Mr. and Mrs. Charles Carmean moved the entire family to a residence on South First Street in Tippecanoe City, Ohio, (presently known as Tipp City) in early 1929. Shortly after moving to that city, she took up with a young man named Charley Boitnott—also from Tipp City—and, much too soon thereafter, in late September of the same year, 1929, the two ran off together to Covington, Kentucky, where they were married. Marguerite's parents, confronted with the fact of their daughter's marriage, permitted them to reside with them in the family home on South First Street until they were able to establish a home of their own in a rental property on South Second Street, just a block or so from Marguerite's parents.

Predictably, the young couple's ill-conceived marriage fared poorly. Because of Boitnott's frequent physical and verbal attacks against her, Marguerite was impelled to leave him in January of 1931, a mere sixteen months after their marriage, and to return to her parents' home. Then, some seven weeks later, in reliance on her husband's assurances that he would conduct himself properly, she returned to him and moved back into their Second Street home. Unhappily, it seems that spousal abusers, like leopards, are constitutionally unable to change their spots, and over the next four months, Charley Boitnott continued to physically attack and to curse his wife, both at home alone with her and in the presence of other persons. Finally, on July 15, Marguerite had endured enough; she moved back to her parents' home and filed an action against her husband for divorce and restraining orders. The matter dragged on for nearly nine months until mid-April of 1932, at which time her petition for divorce was granted, and because there had been no children born as the issue of their marriage, she was restored to her maiden name, Marguerite Carmean.

Court records indicate that Boitnott was thereafter arrested and charged with a series of petty crimes over the next several years, an instructive footnote to the obvious flaws in his character.

As it happened, and as far as we know, Marguerite's fortunes—at least in a romantic context—did not improve after the termination of her disastrous marriage. Her next significant relationship with a person of the opposite sex began in the late summer of 1934 when she became attached to a man named Rollin Cain. Perfectly affable in his manner, he was some two years older than Marguerite, tall and slender, with neatly trimmed dark hair and strong facial features. Although born in nearby Dayton, he had been a lifelong resident of Tippecanoe City. Their relationship began in late August of 1934 and continued through Tuesday, February 19 of 1935.

On that evening, Cain, known to his family as "Tubel," came to Marguerite's home to keep a date that they had arranged over the preceding weekend. Upon his arrival, he was invited into her home and he and Marguerite spent a little time together with her parents. Cain had brought with him the makings of two highballs, which he prepared for Mr. and Mrs. Carmean, and he and Marguerite drank a beer apiece while her parents sipped at their highballs and the four of them sat together around the kitchen table and made small talk. Then, some forty minutes or so later, the young couple borrowed the Carmean's family automobile and drove to the Mac-Mar Club on the South Dixie

Rollin Cain

highway in Montgomery County where they had two glasses of beer apiece and enjoyed the balance of the evening together. Upon leaving the Mac-Mar, they returned to Marguerite's home where they arrived at about midnight and lingered, just inside the front door, long enough to arrange another date for Thursday night. There followed the tender process of parting for the evening and bidding one another goodnight. It had been a pleasant evening and their relationship was an affectionate one, so that there was a fair amount of time spent in a romantic embrace as they held and kissed one another.

At one moment during their embrace, Marguerite thought she'd heard a metallic snap of some order. "What was that?" she inquired.

"Nothing, really," Cain answered quickly. "It was supposed to be a kind of trick—it didn't work very well." He laughed lightly and then re-engaged her in the kissing game. Then, a few moments later, there was a loud explosion and Marguerite sank to the floor, screaming in pain. She'd been shot through the stomach and was bleeding profusely. Cain immediately whirled about and ran out the door.

Both of Marguerite's parents had been wakened by the shot and by Marguerite's screams; they specifically heard her call out, "Mother, come quick." By the time they had rushed from their bedroom and down the stairs, they found their daughter slouched in a chair, her midriff soaked in blood. "Tubel shot me," she gasped hoarsely. "I don't understand it. We hadn't quarreled; he wasn't angry. I have no idea why he did this to me."

"Was he drunk?" demanded her father.

"No, Dad," Marguerite moaned in perplexity. "It was nothing like that. He never drank very much." Then, in an excited, agitated voice, she assured him, "We had just made a date for Thursday and were kissing goodnight. Maybe it was some kind of accident—he seemed as shocked as I was—but then he ran."

A very distressed Charles Carmean made three telephone calls in rapid-fire order, the first such call was to Sheriff's Deputy Howard Frye, who resided in the neighborhood, the second to Dr. F. D. Kaiser, a local physician, and the third to his next-door neighbor, Joe Messick. The latter had already been roused, both by the noise of the gunshot and by Marguerite's screams.

Messick, because he'd had a head start, was the first to arrive, followed in close order by Deputy Frye and Dr. Kaiser. Then, as soon as the situation had been appraised and Dr. Kaiser had made a preliminary assessment of the girl's condition, she was rushed to Stouder Memorial Hospital in nearby Troy, where it was determined that the bullet had passed entirely through her abdomen, puncturing her intestines in four separate places, severing her appendix and exiting through her back. It was reported by hospital personnel that she had little chance of survival. Meanwhile, Deputy Frye had quickly involved both the Miami and Montgomery County sheriff's offices, the village police department and the state highway patrol in a thorough search of the nearby streets and highways. A detailed description of Rollin Cain was broadcast on the state patrol network and the Dayton police radio. All of the authorities believed that Cain was hiding nearby because it was known that he did not drive, had no automobile and no buses had left the village for several hours after the shooting.

Joe Messick had remained on the premises after the family members left to accompany Marguerite to the hospital and he assisted the authorities in their initial examination of the scene. It was he who found the spent bullet under a stand some five or six feet from where Marguerite had collapsed after being shot. It had apparently come to rest there after passing through the girl's body, splintering the edge of a doorframe and bouncing off a wall. He turned it over to Deputy Frye.

From Marguerite's description of the event, the authorities speculated that the shooting had been accidental; that Cain had believed the gun to be unloaded and that he was snapping the hammer in a misguided attempt to tease her. Because he had already pulled the trigger once and laughed when the girl had asked about it, it was thought that he was trying to play some kind of joke. Then, when the gun fired, he must have been as shocked as she was and ran away out of sheer fright.

By midday Wednesday, the search for Rollin Cain had become a full-fledged manhunt; it was obvious that he had somehow managed to elude the local police and sheriff's deputies and that he was no longer in the Tippecanoe area. Marguerite was still in critical condition, but seemed to be holding her own.

Then, late in the evening, Cain casually walked into the police station in Hamilton, Ohio, laid a newspaper account of the shooting on the counter and announced to the officers on duty, "I am the guy, the one they're looking for."

Hamilton Police Officer Clarence Holden stared at Cain with apparent disbelief, then summoned Chief J. C. Calhoun. The two officers questioned Cain briefly in order to satisfy themselves that the man before them was not some attention-seeking crackpot, but a man who was actually attempting to surrender for a crime he had committed. Between them, they decided to inquire further and he was placed under arrest, then taken into Chief Calhoun's office for further questioning.

Referring to the morning edition of the Hamilton newspaper which Cain had brought to the station, Chief Calhoun asked Cain to state his full name and address, together with the name of his victim, his relationship to her and the time and place of the shooting. Cain correctly answered the questions concerning his and Marguerite's identity and their relationship, but added, "I don't have any recollection of a shooting. I don't deny or admit the shooting. I just don't remember."

"Tell us what you do remember?" prompted Calhoun.

Rollin Cain fidgeted, stared off into space, and answered, "Well, I do remember that this last Monday and Tuesday—I'd been drinking pretty hard—I was really kinda messed up, I guess. Anyway, on Monday, I took the bus to Dayton. I stayed that night in a rooming house I'd known about; the next day—Tuesday it was—I just wandered around Dayton awhile. Then I found a pawnshop and bought a handgun and six bullets; paid $2.16 for the lot."

When it seemed to Chief Calhoun that Cain was losing focus, he asked, "Why did you go to Dayton?"

"I don't know."

"Why did you purchase a gun and six bullets?"

Cain looked surprised. "It was a revolver," he answered. "It had six chambers."

"I see," remarked Calhoun. "What I meant was why did you want a gun and ammunition? What did you intend to do with it?"

"I don't know," answered Cain. "I really don't remember."

"Okay, then," Calhoun conceded. "What's the next thing you do remember?"

"I had a date with Marguerite that night—at eight o'clock. So I took the bus back to Tippecanoe and went straight to her house. I remember that I'd brought the fixings for two highballs—her folks like highballs. Then we all sat around the kitchen table while they nursed their drinks; Marguerite and I both had a glass of beer with them and we all just talked awhile."

"Then what?" prompted the chief.

"Well," came the answer haltingly. "I seem to remember that after 45 minutes or so— maybe as long as an hour—Marguerite said we ought to go to a bar some place and leave her folks be. So we took her folks' machine—she drove—and went to a roadhouse on the South Dixie highway. It was toward Dayton."

"Do you remember the name of the roadhouse?"

"Oh, yeah. It's called the Mac-Mar Club. We go there a lot."

"Do you remember how long you stayed there?" asked Calhoun.

"I think we got there a little after 9:00—I don't think we went anywhere else—and left about 11:30 or so."

"Did you have anything to drink at the Mac-Mar?"

"Oh yes, we had two beers apiece."

"Anything else?"

"No, we don't drink any of the hard stuff. We didn't have anything to eat either."

Chief Calhoun was becoming exasperated with the process of wheedling answers from Cain, but he was getting information and had no wish to interrupt his examination. He did, however, excuse himself long enough to instruct another officer to telephone the Miami County Sheriff's office and inform them that they had Cain in custody. Then, he returned to his office and resumed his questioning.

"Alright, Rollin," he coaxed. "Do you remember where you went after you left the Mac-Mar?"

"Yes, sir. We went straight back to Marguerite's home."

"And? What happened next? Do you remember?"

Cain stared at the floor for a short time, then buried his face in his hands. Looking up at Calhoun, he acknowledged, "Actually, Officer, I'm beginning to recollect some of it. I remember that I walked Marguerite to the door like I always do. We went inside and stood by the door to say goodnight. I remember that we agreed on a date for Thursday, and we kissed—we did that several times—and while that was going on, I took the gun out of my coat pocket and put the barrel against her waist and pulled the trigger."

"Why?" asked Calhoun. "Had you been arguing? Weren't you getting along?"

"No, nothing like that," came the indignant answer. "We were getting along fine. I told you we'd just made a date for Thursday."

"Alright, then," continued Calhoun. "Tell me what happened next."

"Actually, nothing happened just then. The gun didn't fire. It just clicked. I heard the hammer fall, but the gun didn't go off. Marguerite heard it too; she asked me what the noise was. I just laughed and told her it was supposed to be a joke, but it didn't work. I slipped the gun back into my pocket without her seeing it, and we went back to kissing and messing around together— you know, kissing and fondling, that sort of thing—she was into it too."

"Then what?" asked Calhoun, his patience beginning to fray.

"Well, like I said, we went back to kissing and stuff, and then, after a while, I took out the gun again and pressed it into her stomach and pulled the trigger. This time it went off—it sounded like a bomb—Marguerite's eyes got real big and she fell to the floor. She was screaming and bleeding like a stuck pig. Worst part of it was she just kept staring at me—never took her eyes off me.

"I got scared and ran out the door. Got clear outta town, fast as I could. I knew her folks woulda heard the shot—God, it was loud—and her screams. Seemed like the whole town had to have heard all the racket. So I ran."

"Where did you run to? How did you get out of town?" pressed Calhoun.

"I walked. I walked to Dayton down the railroad tracks. You know, the B&O runs right through Tippecanoe. I figured there'd be roadblocks set up on all the streets and roads, so I walked the tracks to Dayton. From there I caught a freight train and got here—at Hamilton, I mean—at about four o'clock this afternoon. Then I bought the morning paper and saw what I'd done; I was kinda upset—and confused, too—so I walked around town for an hour or so, trying to get my head straight—I threw the gun into the river—then walked around some more. I finally came here."

Chief Calhoun's examination of Rollin Cain had just about wound itself down when Miami County Prosecuting Attorney Paul Klapp and Sheriff's Chief Deputy Howard Frye arrived and the entire dialogue had had to be repeated for their benefit—and for corroboration. It was obvious to all the officers that Cain's memory of the affair had somehow been fully recovered, if indeed it had ever been impaired, because his repetition of the events of the past three days now appeared to be both detailed and specific. Nonetheless, the one single question he did not—or could not—answer was why he had shot Marguerite in the first place. Both Cain and Marguerite were consistent in their assurances that there had been no argument or contention between them and that their relationship was a mutually affectionate one.

During a private interview with Prosecutor Klapp, Cain was assured that Marguerite was still alive and was actually somewhat improved since the shooting. He also advised Cain that she was greatly mystified over having been shot, inexplicably, by her lover. Rollin Cain still indicated that he had no idea why he'd done what he had and actually suggested to Klapp that he might be insane and that he should probably be examined to determine his mental condition.

Much later that same evening, Cain was taken back to Troy and lodged in the Miami County Jail, where he would be held, without bond, for investigation. It was announced to the press that if Miss Carmean were to die, he would be charged with murder; if she were to survive, he would be charged with shooting with attempt to kill.

2

The following afternoon, Thursday, it was learned that Rollin Cain had retained the Troy law firm of Goodrich & Goodrich to represent him against whatever charges he would face as a result of the shooting. That law firm consisted of fifty-nine-year-old Frank Goodrich, himself a former

Prosecutor Paul T. Klapp

Miami County prosecutor, and his thirty-year-old son, Stanley Goodrich. Both members of the father-son team conferred with Cain briefly just prior to his being further questioned by Assistant Prosecuting Attorney Harley Enyeart. Nothing further was learned about the shooting because Cain, on advice of his newly retained counsel, refused to answer any questions directed to that subject. He did answer questions, with the consent of his counsel, about his movements both before and after the shooting. Enyeart subsequently advised Klapp that Cain seemed unusually clear concerning everything that had occurred—in contrast with his earlier story when he had seemed afflicted with a loss of memory.

During that conference, Cain continued to insist that he and Marguerite had been, at all times, on the best of terms and that there had been no quarrels or other troubles between them.

Harley Enyeart was personally acquainted with Marguerite because he had represented her during her divorce proceedings against Charles Boitnott. Armed with that acquaintanceship and the rapport, which it implied, it was he who interviewed her later that afternoon. He found her condition to be much improved and that there was good reason to be optimistic about her chances of making a full recovery. She confirmed that there had been no difficulties between her and Cain and that she had no idea as to the motive for his having shot her.

In his report to Prosecutor Klapp that evening, the ever-sardonic Enyeart remarked, "I don't, for one goddamn minute, believe either one of them on that score. People don't just shoot one another for no reason."

Although only twenty-seven years old and only recently elected as Prosecuting Attorney, Paul Klapp was the epitome of everything one might expect of a capable and highly respected prosecutor. He was tall, lean, and well dressed, with a full mane of prematurely white hair, and his manners were impeccable. Now, he seemed deep in thought as he digested Enyeart's report. "I couldn't agree more," he said. "And it most certainly wasn't a spur-of-the-moment thing, a sudden impulse. Remember, he admitted that he'd ridden a bus to and from Dayton earlier in the week just to buy a gun and ammunition."

"And if that doesn't constitute both malice and premeditation, I can't imagine what might," added Enyeart.

"And intent," appended Klapp. "If the girl dies, we'll have a clear case of first degree murder."

"The hell of it is, we may never know the *why* of it," said Enyeart. "There's a whole lot more to this thing than anyone is telling us—or that we may ever know."

Not surprisingly, and despite Thursday's apparent improvement in her condition, Marguerite Carmean died at 12:30 a.m. Saturday morning, and, at Paul Klapp's request, County Coroner Cecil Marshall conducted an immediate inquest and ordered an autopsy to be performed by Drs. B. M. Hogle, J. S. Shinn, F. D. Kaiser and S. F. Yenger, the latter a pathologist from Sidney, Ohio. The autopsy report, as anticipated, gave as the primary cause of death the gunshot wound to the abdomen, which had punctured her intestines in four places and severed her appendix, together with infectious peritonitis caused by the leakage of the intestinal contents into her abdominal cavity. A secondary cause was reported as aggravation of a heart condition occasioned by systemic toxicity, which had resulted from the bowel leakage.

Because Marguerite's death had occurred over the weekend when the courts were closed, it was Monday morning before an affidavit charging Rollin Cain with first-degree murder could be filed against him as a first item of business. It was signed by Deputy Howard Frye and filed at the direction of Prosecuting Attorney Paul Klapp. Cain was immediately arraigned in the court of Justice of the Peace Leo Gross where, flanked by his attorneys, he entered a plea of "Not guilty." Justice Gross remanded him to the county jail, to be held without bond, and scheduled the matter for preliminary hearing on March 1.

Upon his return to the county jail, Rollin Cain promptly made it known that he would refuse to see any visitors other than his attorneys and members of his immediate family. And when two of his Tippecanoe acquaintances attempted to visit him, he informed his jailors that he didn't know them and would not, under any circumstances, consent to speak with them.

And though he was confined on the first floor of the jail along with a number of other prisoners, he would have nothing to do with any of them. He became increasingly moody and spent virtually all his time sitting by himself, staring into space and apparently brooding over what he had done.

There may be some small irony in the fact that at the precise moment of Cain's arraignment, a brief funeral service was held for Marguerite in the family home in Tippecanoe, following which her body was taken to Noblesville, Indiana for burial.

On the Wednesday prior to the March 1 preliminary hearing date, Deputy Sheriffs Howard Frye and Tony Berberick spent the entire day in the vicinity of the High Street bridge in Hamilton, dragging the Miami River in what proved to be a futile attempt to recover the revolver that Cain had said he'd tossed into the stream from the center of the bridge. Despite the fact that they were assisted in their efforts by a crew of Hamilton's local law officials and used extra-long-handled rakes and an exceptionally powerful magnet, they were unable to recover the gun. The deputies ultimately abandoned the search with the belief that *if indeed* Cain had truly thrown the gun into the stream at that place, as he claimed, it was probably carried downstream by the extraordinarily swift current resulting from the heavy spring rains.

The preliminary hearing to determine whether there existed probable cause to hold Cain to the grand jury was held, as scheduled, on March 1, in the Common Pleas Courtroom in Troy's stately, 70-odd-year-old courthouse. Justice Leo Gross again presided. Although conducted formally and in accordance with law, it turned out to be much in the nature of a non-event. The State offered the testimony of only six witnesses. Deputy Sheriff Frye, and Tippecanoe's Village Marshal J. W. Brown and night Police Officer Robert Thomas, all testified as to their investigations on the night of the murder and the admissions made by Cain in their presence. County Coroner Cecil Marshall and Drs. Hogle and Kaiser told of their findings at the inquest and upon the post-mortem examination of Marguerite Carmean. Cain's attorneys, Goodrich & Goodrich cross-examined the State's witnesses thoroughly, but offered no testimony on behalf of the Defendant. The result of the hearing was, at all times, a foregone conclusion. Justice Gross was constrained by law to bind Cain over to the next session of the grand jury on the charge of murder in the first degree.

Cain himself had taken no part in the proceedings and appeared no more than slightly interested in any of the testimony. He sat in his assigned seat, flanked by his attorneys, and spent the entire time staring moodily at the floor in front of him or covering his face with his hands. He did speak briefly with his father and sister and with his attorneys before being returned to jail to await action by the grand jury.

In the ordinary course of events the next session of the grand jury would have been held the first week in May, but because that was nearly two months in the future, Prosecutor Klapp convened the same on Tuesday, March 12 to consider the Cain murder charge and a number of lesser charges against some 14 other alleged miscreants. Four days later, on the sixteenth, the grand jury filed its report with Judge Walter D. Jones; it contained a total of thirteen indictments for various felony charges, including an indictment against Rollin Cain charging—in the arcane language of the law—that:

> *....on the twentieth day of February in the year of our Lord one thousand nine hundred and thirty-five, at the county of Miami aforesaid, one Rollin Cain, did unlawfully, purposely and of deliberate and premeditated malice, kill Marguerite Carmean.*
>
> *Contrary to the statute in such case made and provided, and against the peace and dignity of the State of Ohio.*

Rollin Cain next appeared in Judge Jones's court on March 25, together with Stanley Goodrich, and the two men, the accused and his counsel, stood at the bar while Clerk of Courts Brooks Johnson read the indictment charging him with murder in the first degree. The Defendant quietly entered a plea of "Not guilty" and was forthwith remanded to the custody of the sheriff to await trial.

Then, by order journalized on April 1, trial on the merits was scheduled to begin on Monday, April 22 and the Clerk was ordered to cause a special venire of seventy-five jurors to be drawn from the jury wheel and summoned to appear for trial.

3

Shortly before Rollin Cain's trial date rolled around, it was learned that long-time Miami County Common Pleas Court, Judge Walter D. Jones, would be unavailable to preside, and because of that fact, the Supreme Court of Ohio appointed forty-four-year-old Judge Lowell C. Bodey of nearby Champaign County to replace him on the Miami County bench for purposes of the Cain trial. Bodey was a fair-minded, no-nonsense judge who had a well-deserved reputation for controlling his courtrooms and was often assigned to substitute for indisposed judges in nearby counties.

The usual procedure by which jurors were selected in criminal cases was, until the adoption of Ohio's new criminal rules, to place the first twelve veniremen in the jury box and question them as a group. By reason of the adoption of the new rules, it was necessary for Judge Bodey to segregate the veniremen, then call them, one by one, into the courtroom so that he and the lawyers could then examine them separately as to his or her qualifications to serve in this specific case. As each prospective juror took the witness stand and swore to answer truthfully, Judge Bodey, in accordance with the new rules, first questioned them as to their prior knowledge of the case itself and/or the parties and their respective counsel. He also questioned them as to whether or not they were opposed to the death penalty as a matter of principle. One of the veniremen drew

Judge Bodey

a round of laughter from the sparsely occupied spectators' section when he responded to Judge Bodey's questioning to the effect that he did, indeed, believe in capital punishment, "but only in cases like that of John Dillinger or other gangsters of that type." When the laughter finally subsided, Judge Bodey politely excused the man and asked the bailiff to escort the next venireman into the courtroom.

Then, having satisfied himself of such matters—as to each prospective juror—the judge next invited counsel for the parties to pose such additional questions to each of them as they felt appropriate. It was clearly apparent from Paul Klapp's questioning that he fully intended to demand the imposition of the death penalty for the Defendant. Very little concerning the line of defense could be inferred from Frank Goodrich's questions; his examination of each was essentially routine and perfunctory. He did make a point of inquiring of each whether it would make any difference to them that the Defendant's alleged victim was a young woman. Harley Enyeart was heard to snarl in the Prosecutor's direction, "What the hell difference does that make?" before being shushed by Klapp and incurring a harsh look from Judge Bodey.

All in all, however, the process ran smoothly and efficiently. A jury of eight women and four men was seated, sworn and admonished by the end of the day.

"Where in hell is Goodrich leading with that dumb line of questioning?" asked Enyeart after court had adjourned for the day and he and Klapp were closeted together in the Prosecutor's office.

"Damned if I know," answered Klapp. "Your guess is as good as mine. Better, actually, you've been in this business a lot longer than I have."

"Well, then," said Enyeart. "If I'm to make a guess, I'll guess that he's already realized that there's no way in hell he can get an acquittal, and he's angling for a life sentence."

"Explain that for me, would you?" asked Klapp. "I don't see the connection."

"My guess is that he's convinced himself that if he keeps reminding the jury that they should take care not to send this bastard to the chair just because he killed a *poor, defenseless woman*, they'll recommend mercy just to preserve the illusion of fairness. I see it as a bit of reverse psychology."

"Sounds like a dangerous strategy to me," mused Paul Klapp.

"Mmmhmm," mumbled Enyeart. "But what else has he got?"

"Insanity?" suggested Klapp.

"Might have worked, but..."

"But they didn't plead it," Klapp finished the thought.

"Wonder why not. Why wouldn't they have pleaded it?" mused Enyeart.

"Ours not to reason why... " answered Klapp. "Maybe the bard was right."

"The bard." repeated Enyeart. "Shakespeare?"

"Tennyson," Klapp reminded. "It's been a long day."

4

As a first item of business on the second day of trial, the jury was taken to the Carmean home in Tippecanoe City for the traditional "jury view" of the scene of the crime. In a somewhat unusual twist, and out of the presence of the jury, Judge Bodey directed Cain to demonstrate the place and position in which he had been standing while bidding Marguerite goodnight. He was also asked to indicate the girl's position. Cain did as he was instructed, but did so hesitantly and with obvious repressed emotion. He kept his head bowed and declined to look at either the judge or his attorneys during the entire time.

Then, after he had complied with Judge Bodey's instructions, Cain was permitted to retire to an adjoining room and the jury was led into the house where the events of the alleged crime were actually re-enacted for their benefit, with Sheriff Kenny Miller assuming the place and the role of Cain and Deputy Frye assuming that of Marguerite. Deputy Frye was permitted to explain to the jury that their respective placements and actions represented those of the actual participants in the shooting. He also explained the location of the various items of furniture in the room and pointed out the splintering of the doorframe and the hole made in the plaster by the bullet before it had fallen to the floor.

Directly after the jury view of the premises and the re-enactment of the alleged crime, the jury was taken back to the courtroom and Paul Klapp made a somewhat protracted opening statement in which he explained to the jury, in great detail, precisely what it was that he expected the evidence to show concerning the Defendant's activities before, during and after the shooting of Miss Carmean.

Frank Goodrich caused a ripple of surprise in the courtroom when he declined the opportunity to make an opening statement. He simply advised the jury that the Defendant had entered a plea of "Not guilty" to the charge—and resumed his seat at the counsel table.

Thomas C. Freshour, a deputy county engineer, was the first witness called by the State. In response to Paul Klapp's questioning, he explained a detailed drawing he had made of the interior of the Carmean home. There was no cross-examination and his drawing was admitted into evidence without objection.

The second prosecution witness was Robert Thomas. He was a night policeman for Tippecanoe City and told the jury of his having been called to the Carmean residence after the shooting and of his initial investigation. He also attempted to tell of his conversation that evening with Marguerite when she had told him that Cain had shot her, but that testimony was excluded on objection by Goodrich. Judge Bodey ruled that any testimony as to what Marguerite had told him was inadmissible under the so-called "hearsay rule" and not within the "dying declaration" exception to that rule because she could not have known she was dying at the time.

"That's bullshit," Enyeart whispered to Klapp, as Judge Bodey dismissed the jury for lunch. "It's admissible as a part of the *res*; it's also an excited utterance. Either way, it's admissible."

"Don't worry about it, Harley, " answered Klapp. "We don't need it."

The flow of incriminating evidence against Rollin Cain picked up momentum during the next day and a half. The next two witnesses called to the stand were Marguerite's parents, Mr. and Mrs. Charles Carmean. Both told of their having heard the shot, followed by their daughter's screams, and their having found her slumped in a chair, bleeding profusely, and both told of her having said that "Tubel" had shot her. Their testimony was entirely consistent, one with the other, and they both showed signs of repressed emotion. Mrs.

Carmean nearly broke down when asked by Klapp to identify the bloodstained clothing worn by her daughter on the night of the shooting. Both of her parents told the jury that Marguerite had reiterated to them that Cain was not drunk and had not seemed angry, and that she had said she had no idea why he had shot her.

"Whatever happened to the hearsay rule?" whispered Enyeart when Klapp had finished his examinations and resumed his seat at the counsel table. "We didn't even hear an objection this time."

"Can't imagine," returned Klapp. "It's precisely the same testimony that Bodey excluded from Frye's examination this morning when Frank objected."

"I suspect," whispered Enyeart, "that one or both of them had a hard look at the hearsay rule over the lunch hour."

Frank Goodrich's cross-examination of each of Marguerite's parents consisted of one single question, "Are you quite positive that there had been no trouble between your daughter and Mr. Cain that evening?"

And each of them answered emphatically they didn't know of any trouble or arguments between the two of them during their six-month relationship.

Joe Messick, the Carmeans' next-door neighbor, followed them to the witness stand. He also told the jury of his having heard the shot and Marguerite's screams. He added that it was he who had found the spent slug under a stand, where it had apparently come to rest after splintering the doorframe and bouncing off a wall.

Dr. F. D. Kaiser was next called to the stand to describe the injuries he had observed and to explain the findings on autopsy. It came as no surprise to anyone that he declared the cause of death to be infectious peritonitis resulting from the several perforations of the bowel by the Defendant's bullet.

He was followed by Drs. Russell Gardner, J. S. Shinn and Berton M. Hogle of Troy and by Dr. S. F. Yinger, the Sidney pathologist, all of whom confirmed the testimony of Dr. Kaiser as to the injuries inflicted by the fatal bullet. In his cross-examination of the doctors, Stanley Goodrich strenuously attempted to induce each or any one of them, to concede the possibility that Marguerite Carmean just might have died from causes unrelated to her having been mortally wounded by the Defendant. The suggestion was patently ludicrous and the only thing he accomplished by his efforts was to make himself look ridiculous.

5

Then, on Wednesday morning, beginning in rapid-fire, if somewhat tedious order, came Chief Calhoun and William Welch of the Hamilton Police Department, State Patrolman E. R. Davis and Miami County Sheriff Kenneth Miller, all of whom testified concerning Cain's having surrendered himself and the statements he had made to them, or in their presence, at the time. Job Brown, village Marshall for Tippecanoe City was next called to the stand. He testified that he had made the trip to Hamilton to bring Cain back to Miami County and had heard him acknowledge the statements he had earlier made to the officers, and had, in fact, been one of the four persons who had later signed the written statement as witnesses.

"Actually," Brown said on direct examination by Klapp, "during the trip back to Troy, Cain told me that he had bought the gun the day before for the purpose of shooting Miss Carmean and that he shot her because they'd been drifting apart and were not as close as they had been."

The next witness, Deputy Howard Frye, told the jury that he had made a trip to Dayton to retrieve Cain's suitcase, packed with clothing, from a locker at the bus station where Cain had told him he had left it on the day before the shooting. More to the point, Frye also confirmed Cain's admissions to the officers and added to the mix that Cain had told him privately that he had intended shooting Miss Carmean and then committing suicide, but that he had lost his nerve after wounding her.

An additional corroborative witness was called by the State. He was identified as Bert Shroyer, a Dayton pawnbroker. After consulting his records, he testified that on the afternoon of February 19 he had sold a .32 caliber revolver to a man who had given his name and address as George Hetzler of 234 South Walnut Street, Troy, Ohio. Then, upon being asked if he could identify "Mr. Hetzler," the pawnbroker stepped down from the witness stand, walked across the courtroom and placed his hand on the Defendant's shoulder. By way of support for his testimony, he offered his sales record book and pointed to the entry memorializing the sale. At Paul Klapp's request, the book was admitted into evidence.

When Paul Klapp finally offered Cain's written statement into evidence, his effort was met with strenuous objections by both Frank and Stanley Goodrich. The statement was not voluntarily made, they insisted, and could not be viewed, heard or considered by the jury. No sooner had the objections been made, than Judge Bodey excused the jury in order that the lawyers might conduct their arguments on the objections out of the hearing of the jurors.

Frank Goodrich argued that the proffered statement could not be considered as voluntary because all of the admissions contained therein were given in response to questions put to the Defendant by police officers while he was in custody. Paul Klapp countered Goodrich's arguments by pointing out that the Defendant had not been arrested and was not, therefore, in custody when he made his admissions to the Hamilton officials; that he had not been threatened or forced in any manner to answer the questions. Additionally, Klapp pointed out that after Cain had made the statement and been returned to Troy, he had re-read the same, admitted that it was true and correct, and voluntarily signed it in the office of the Miami County jail.

Judge Bodey, having heard the arguments, ruled the confession to have been voluntary and admitted the same into evidence. The jury was called back into the courtroom and Paul Klapp was permitted to read the Defendant's statement to them. It provided that:

> *I, Rollin Cain, make this statement of my own free will and without any coercion or threats or promises made to me.*
>
> *On Monday, February 18, 1935, I went to Dayton from Tippecanoe City and took a room on Jefferson Street. On Tuesday I bought a revolver, .32 caliber, and six cartridges for same. I came to Tippecanoe City, Tuesday night, February 19, 1935, and kept a date with Marguerite Carmean at her home on South First Street, Tippecanoe City, which I had previously made with her. We went to the Mac-Mar Club on the Dixie Highway and had two glasses of beer each; then we returned to the Carmean home. When I left the Carmean home about*

twelve o'clock Tuesday night, I shot Marguerite with the revolver I had purchased. We had not been quarreling, and I don't know why I shot her. I left Tippecanoe City and walked to Dayton on the B&O Railway tracks. I stayed in Dayton until noon on Wednesday when I caught a freight train to Hamilton, Ohio. At Hamilton I went to police headquarters and gave myself up. The foregoing statement is true and correct.

> *(Signed) ROLLIN CAIN*
> *Witnesses----*
> *Kenneth Miller*
> *E. R. Davis*
> *Howard Frye*
> *J. W. Brown*

Whatever impression Rollin Cain's statement may have had on the eight women and four men seated in the jury box, it most certainly had a palpable impact on the spectators in the courtroom. After an initial stunned silence, a collective gasp of mingled shock, disbelief and anger emanated from the rapt assemblage who—in contradistinction from Monday's scanty numbers—had, by the end of Tuesday's session, packed the gallery to overflowing. The dramatic escalation of public interest in the proceedings was in no small way attributable to the extensive newspaper coverage accorded by all of the newspapers within the southern part of the state, all of which had dubbed the matter as "The Kiss-Killer Case." Now, late in the day on Wednesday, even the corridors outside the courtroom were jam-packed by interested persons hoping either to gain entrance into the crowded gallery or to learn of what was transpiring within the courtroom. Judge Bodey banged his gavel repeatedly and threatened to have the bailiff clear the courtroom—and the corridors—until sufficient order was restored to enable the proceedings to continue.

Then, when order had finally been restored, Paul Klapp moved the introduction of the State's exhibits, and formally announced, "The State rests, Your Honor."

And, because it was late in the day, Frank Goodrich requested that the Court adjourn until the following morning, at which time the Defendant's case would be presented. Judge Bodey granted the request, admonished the jury and adjourned court for the day.

"Well," declared an exhausted Klapp during his post-session conference with Enyeart, "the gallery certainly got its money's worth these last two days."

"They sure as hell did," answered Enyeart. "In addition to yesterday's murder re-enactment, we got through seventeen witnesses, and a signed, sealed and delivered confession from the Defendant. What more could they have asked?"

"How 'bout a touch of comic relief?" suggested Klapp.

"Yeah, they even got a touch of that," conceded Enyeart. "I'd give twenty dollars for a photograph of the look on Judge Bodey's face when you asked Officer Davis to point out Cain to the jury, and he stared at Bodey so long and hard I was just sure he was going to identify him as the Defendant."

"Me too," laughed Klapp. "And, judging from Bodey's expression and the burst of laughter from the crowd, I think everybody else thought so too."

"I'm just glad he got it straight and finally pointed to Cain. We don't really want a misidentification like that on the record."

Klapp produced a bottle and a pair of jelly glasses and the two men wasted a moment or so sipping and chuckling over Judge Bodey's discomfiture—and their own apprehensions—when it had appeared that Officer Davis was about to inculpate His Honor as a murderer.

Ultimately, their mood became more professional as they reviewed the last two days' proceedings. "On balance," opined Klapp, "It went well. We've made our case; our evidence and our exhibits are all in. Have we missed anything?"

"Don't think so," said Enyeart. "So far, so good. But I think we need to stay awake. We don't really know what Goodrich has up his sleeve. He hasn't given us a clue yet, and that concerns me."

"You're right," agreed Klapp. "He didn't give notice of *alibi*, he didn't plead insanity or irresistible impulse, and he made no opening statement. As of this moment we have no indication whatever as to what his defense is likely to be."

"He's subpoenaed seven witnesses," remarked Enyeart, "just family members and friends, but we can't really deduce much from that. We've been looking at his parents, his brother and sister every day this week, but that doesn't give us much of a clue as to his defense."

"Yeah," agreed Klapp, "we've been looking at them, but I doubt if Cain has even seen them—or anybody else for that matter. Have you been watching him these last few days? He hasn't said a word to any of them—not even a 'hello', 'goodbye' or 'kiss my foot.' I haven't seen him look at anyone or anything, other than the floor, all week."

"Hell, I've not seen him speak with either of his attorneys either," added Enyeart. "I doubt seriously if there's anyone in the courtroom—or anywhere else—who's seemed less interested in what's happening in the trial than has our Mr. Cain."

"That says it all. He's been virtually catatonic."

"So, Mr. Prosecutor," pressed Enyeart caustically, "how the hell do we prepare for cross-examination? We've already acknowledged that we have no idea what they're likely to testify about."

"I guess we just play it by ear," Klapp conceded. "Except as to Cain himself. We can certainly prepare for that."

"Do you really expect him to take the stand?" asked Enyeart.

"Well, I hadn't," came the answer. "But Frank told me, just this afternoon, that Cain is likely to be his first witness."

Enyeart snorted. "I don't believe that for a minute. If we haven't already convicted him, he'll do it himself inside the first twenty minutes."

6

On Thursday morning, Rollin Cain's sister, Ruth Becker, appeared at the county jail prior to starting time for the morning court session. Knowing that her brother was to take the stand in his own defense, she had wanted to encourage him and to reassure him of her confidence in his innocence. Then, when it came time for Sheriff Miller to take him across the street to the county courthouse, Mrs. Becker was permitted to walk alongside her brother. It was on that occasion that Cain leaned in close to his sister's ear and whispered, "Ruthie, I have to tell you I can't stand another day of this. I just can't."

"Oh, Tubel, it'll all be over soon. I'm sure you'll be acquitted and we can all go home. All you have to do is hold on for another hour or two—tell your side of the story—and everything'll be just fine."

"I'm not gonna do it, Ruth. I can't. My lawyers have been telling me all week that I have to take the stand and defend myself, but I just can't do it. I won't do it," he said forcefully.

"But, Tubel, just thin..."

"No. No. No," he insisted. "They can do whatever they want to me; they can drag me to the witness chair, but they can't make me say a word."

"Tubel, please..." she pleaded.

"I won't. That's all there is to it."

Moments later, they entered the courtroom. Judge Bodey was already seated at the bench, Paul Klapp and Harley Enyeart were standing at their counsel table, ordering their papers for the morning session, and the Defendant's counsel, Frank and Stanley Goodrich, rose to greet their client. Sheriff Miller removed the handcuffs from Cain's wrists in accordance with the established procedure in order that the jury not be prejudiced by the appearance of the Defendant in shackles.

Miami County Jail

As soon as his client was seated, Stan Goodrich asked Judge Bodey to delay the bailiff's seating of the jury and to permit him and his father to adjourn to the law library, located just across the hall next to the Prosecutor's office, for a ten-minute conference with their client. Judge Bodey granted the request, and the Messrs. Goodrich led their client through the doorway next to the vacant jury box and into the central corridor outside the courtroom.

Then, as soon as they had cleared the doorway, Rollin Cain made a break for the wide, double stairway at the west end of the building. His sister screamed to him to stop, and as he ran toward the stairwell, he passed his mother who was seated by the stair railing. She realized immediately that her son was attempting to escape, saw Sheriff Miller reach for his gun and start to chase him, and began to scream hysterically, "Stop, Tubel, stop! Sheriff, don't shoot!"

Cain leapt to the mid-floor landing, turned the corner and attempted a similar leap in the opposite direction from there to the second floor below. Sheriff Miller followed in close pursuit and made the same leap to the landing, drawing his handgun in the process and demanding that the Defendant stop. Then, just before Cain landed at the bottom of the stairs, the sheriff fired a single shot, and Cain stumbled and nearly fell.

He hadn't been hit, but had sprained his ankle when he landed after his second leap. The brief hesitation occasioned by his stumble was sufficient to allow the pursuing deputies—and those who had descended from the east stairways—to lay hands on him, and a furious battle ensued until five or six of the sheriff's deputies managed to subdue him long enough to handcuff and thoroughly shackle him. Still struggling violently, he was then half-dragged, half-carried back to the county jail.

It had all happened in less than a minute, but it had most certainly wreaked havoc within the courthouse and its immediate environs. The noise of Sheriff Miller's single shot reverberated throughout the building; the women's screaming and that of the spectators in the crowded courtroom was deafening and contributed immensely to the chaos that reigned until Cain had been recaptured and confined under heavy guard at the jail. Courthouse personnel, not having been aware of precisely what the commotion was about, had dived under desks, tables and whatever else was perceived to offer some sort of protective cover.

All in all, it had been a harrowing exercise; in its aftermath, Cain's mother, sobbing uncontrollably, had to be returned to her home and his sister's nerves had been shattered. Both had initially believed that Cain had been wounded, perhaps mortally, by Sheriff Miller's single shot.

Before order could be restored, one of the sheriff's deputies reported to the Court and counsel that Cain had been painstakingly searched upon his return to the jail and that their search had yielded up two separate weapons hidden in his clothing. The first item, which was discovered in his inside coat pocket, was a dagger which had obviously been fashioned from a spoon and sharpened against the prison wall to an extraordinary sharpness; the second item was a razor blade, wrapped in a cigarette paper, and hidden in his shirt pocket. The officers speculated that Cain had armed himself so that he could commit suicide if his attempt to escape had failed. He had also told the officers that he had intended to be shot to death in the attempt. That, he'd insisted, was what he had wanted to happen.

As he sat in a straight chair in the sheriff's office waiting to be summoned back to the courtroom, Cain complained to Sheriff Miller, "These handcuffs are too tight, they're chafing my wrists. Can't you take them off?"

And Miller swiftly replied, "No, I can't. I'm sorry you're uncomfortable, but I've got reason to believe you'll try to escape again, and I really don't want to have to shoot you." He winked at one of his deputies and continued lightly, "Who knows? This time I might even hit you."

"That's what I want," pleaded Cain. "I want you to kill me."

7

As soon as some semblance of order had been restored in the courtroom, and before the jury had been reseated, Judge Bodey informed counsel that he considered himself duty-bound to inform the jury of the Defendant's attempted escape and his swift recapture. Frank Goodrich asked that the Judge declare a mistrial, arguing that in view of the morning's events, it was no longer possible for him to receive a fair trial. "The attempt itself will undoubtedly prejudice the jury against the Defendant," he urged. "Besides, we had intended to put him on the stand to testify in his own behalf. Clearly, we can no longer do that, and that fact alone seriously undermines our ability to properly defend him in this proceeding."

"Motion denied," responded Judge Bodey. "I recognize that the Defendant's attempt to escape may very well influence the jury; I also recognize that his conduct has most certainly had an adverse effect on your ability to properly defend him. However, it cannot be denied that the situation has been of the Defendant's own making, and he must answer for the consequences of his actions. The trial will continue."

The two Goodrichs, father and son, put their heads together for a short conference at the counsel table. After Stanley nodded affirmatively, Frank Goodrich rose and addressed Judge Bodey and, by extension, the two prosecutors. "If it please the Court, as counsel for the Defendant, we appreciate the Court's recognition of the situation in which we now find ourselves and the immeasurable damage wreaked upon Mr. Cain's defense by his improvident conduct this morning. We also respectfully accept the Court's ruling on our motion for mistrial.

"And because of the present posture of the matter, we are, at this time, prepared to offer, on behalf of the Defendant, a plea of guilty to murder in the second degree."

Judge Bodey looked askance at Paul Klapp and Harley Enyeart. Klapp promptly rose to his feet and advised Court and counsel that the offer was unacceptable. "The Defendant is demonstrably guilty of murder in the first degree. He has admitted it, and we have proved it. His actions of this morning simply fortify the State's case and underscore the enormity of his crime.

"However," he continued, "because both the circumstances of the crime and the Defendant's deportment throughout the four days of trial would seem to indicate that his mental condition, both now and then, has been somewhat abnormal, the State will accept a plea of guilty to murder in the first degree, *with a recommendation of mercy*. If that is unacceptable to the Defense, then the State will insist on proceeding to verdict."

At that point in the proceedings, Judge Bodey interceded. "As all of you know, I cannot accept the Defendant's plea without the State's consent. I would point out that both the plea offered by the Defendant—and that demanded by the State—carry the same penalty, life imprisonment. I would also comment, gratuitously, I acknowledge, that the Defendant appears to suffer from some mental deficiency or disease, and should be evaluated. With all those considerations in mind, I would urge counsel to confer among themselves concerning the matter."

Judge Bodey shifted his gaze from Klapp to the Goodrichs, and back again. "It's now 11:30. We will recess until 2:30 this afternoon, at which time, the trial will resume. I am hopeful that the four of you, all of whom I regard as capable and reasonable lawyers, will utilize the intervening period of time to resolve your issues and resolve the matter in some mutually agreeable fashion."

Three hours later, at precisely 2:30 in the afternoon, Judge Bodey entered the courtroom through the Clerk's office and made his way to his padded swivel chair behind the dais. Rollin Cain, his feet hobbled and his wrists cuffed to his waist, flanked by his attorneys and surrounded by a corps of deputies, stood at the defense counsel table and stared dejectedly at the floor. Paul Klapp and Harley Enyeart, both wearing stern, unyielding expressions on their faces, stood stoically at their counsel table. The largest crowd of onlookers ever known to have filled the gallery, the doorways and the corridors likewise remained standing until Judge Bodey had assumed his seat, nodded to Cliff Blair, the court stenographer, and invited the entire assemblage to be seated.

Judge Bodey then formally re-opened court for the afternoon session. "Let the record show that I have been advised by counsel for the parties that they have been unable to reach an agreement to resolve this matter," he announced, "and that the trial must, therefore, continue." He then inquired of counsel, "Have I stated the matter correctly?"

When each of the four lawyers had affirmed that he had, indeed, correctly stated the present posture of the case, Judge Bodey inquired further, "Anything else, before we call the jury in?"

"One thing, Your Honor," responded Frank Goodrich. "Despite the fact that we have been unable to agree concerning a plea by the Defendant, I would like the record to reflect—out of the presence of the jury—that the

Defendant now formally offers to enter a plea of 'guilty' to the included offense of murder in the second degree. As the Court is aware, our prior offer of such a plea has been rejected by the State and Counsel has demanded a plea of 'guilty' to the charge of murder in the first degree, with a recommendation of mercy. Nonetheless, for the purposes of the record, the Defendant has requested that we now renew the prior offer.

"In support of the Defendant's offer, and in the hope that the State will reconsider its position, I should like to reiterate—one more time—that the penalty mandated by statute, for either charge, is precisely the same, life imprisonment. A guilty plea to either charge will subject the Defendant to the same punishment and will therefore adequately protect the public from further depredations at the hands of the Defendant.

"I am quite certain that both the Court and counsel for the State have noted the Defendant's demeanor during the past four days; although his very life has been at stake since the inception of the matter, he has appeared entirely uninterested in the proceedings and has refused to communicate meaningfully with either his family or his counsel. We submit that his conduct— especially in the light of this morning's episode—has been abnormal. It must also be obvious to everyone that the Defendant himself is not normal. We have offered this plea—to murder in the second degree in the hope that he may be sent to Lima State Hospital for the criminally insane for psychiatric evaluation and treatment. And, if he is found to be presently sane—or should he ultimately be cured—he could then be transferred to the Ohio State Penitentiary with the possibility of eventual parole.

"On behalf of the Defendant—and his family—we respectfully submit that such a denouement would adequately serve the ends of justice. We only ask that such justice be tempered with mercy."

Judge Bodey asked Rollin Cain to stand and, when the tautly fettered Defendant had managed to do so, he asked, "Mr. Cain, you have heard your attorney's offer and his supporting remarks; is it your desire to plead guilty to a charge of murder in the second degree?"

Cain responded in a steady voice, "It is."

"You now tell this Court that you are guilty of murder in the second degree?" asked Bodey again.

"Yes, sir."

Judge Bodey then turned his attention to the Prosecutors' table and nodded. It was an invitation to the State to respond. Paul Klapp conferred briefly with Harley Enyeart, then rose and addressed the Court, "If it please the Court, up until this moment, we have steadfastly refused to accept the Defendant's offer. However, we now find ourselves convinced by the remarks of defense counsel—and by the several considerations to which he alluded—that it is in the best interests of the State of Ohio that the Defendant's plea be accepted.

"That decision has not been lightly made. We must recognize that the Defendant's deportment—as well as his actions this morning—strongly suggest that he may indeed suffer from some sort of mental disease or deficiency. We have suspected that such might be the case from the date of the crime itself and recent developments have confirmed those suspicions.

"We also recognize that the Defendant's plea to second degree murder carries precisely the same penalty as does first degree, *accompanied by a recommendation of mercy*—which the State had previously offered. We have consistently felt that if any error should be made with reference to this matter, such an error should be on the side of mercy.

"And finally, we have considered the terrible anguish occasioned to the family members of the Defendant and the victim; we have no desire to inflict further pain on those persons by prolonging these proceedings further than necessary.

"The Defendant's plea is accepted."

The fully packed courtroom had been preternaturally quiet throughout the entirety of the afternoon proceedings as everyone present strained to hear the remarks of both counsel. Then, as soon as Paul Klapp's surprise acceptance of the Defendant's plea had registered with the crowd, a fully spontaneous round of applause filled the chamber. It began with no more than a handful of diffident claps of approval and ultimately grew into a standing, cheering ovation. Judge Bodey permitted the demonstration to run on for some four or five minutes before he banged his gavel and called for order. There was still some business to attend to before the proceedings were completely over. Although Paul Klapp was the Prosecutor and therefore lead counsel for the State, Judge Bodey inquired of Assistant Prosecutor Harley Enyeart as to whether he concurred with Klapp's remarks and his acceptance of the plea.

Enyeart struggled to his feet, both hands gripping the counsel table for support and answered affirmatively, "I do, Your Honor. And from the demonstration we just witnessed, it appears that everyone else here agrees as well. I think acceptance of the plea is in the best interests of all of the parties. Justice has been served."

At Judge Bodey's direction, the bailiff then dutifully escorted the jury back into the courtroom and caused them to re-seat themselves in the box. Judge Bodey then advised the jury as to the day's events and the ultimate agreement of the parties. He expressed to them that he approved their agreement and had formally accepted the plea. "That concludes the proceedings and, with the sincere thanks of the Court for your service, you are hereby dismissed."

Both Paul Klapp and Frank Goodrich added their own thanks to the members of the jury panel, and the bailiff then escorted them out of the courtroom. The spectators abandoned their seats in the gallery and such other vantage points as they had achieved, and, within a matter of perhaps twenty minutes, the chamber was cleared, except for the trial participants, all of whom had remained at their respective stations. Court was still in session, but only to attend to the remaining details.

"Tell you what," Judge Bodey began in a less formal manner than had prevailed during the trial itself. "If Defense counsel will be good enough to secure and file a certificate from a reputable physician to the effect that the Defendant is probably insane, I will issue an order directing him to be removed to Lima State Hospital, to be held for thirty days for observation and evaluation, and I will defer sentencing him until we have their report and evaluation in hand."

Frank Gingrich then rose to his feet and responded, "Court please, we have already consulted with Dr. Gardner and he has indicated to us that he will provide such a certificate forthwith."

And, within the hour, the Messrs. Goodrich filed their own representation, as counsel, to the effect that the Defendant was not then sane; that representation was accompanied by a medical certificate, signed by Dr. Russell Gardner, certifying that he had examined the Defendant for the purpose of determining whether or not he was then sane and concluding with "... it is my opinion that Rollin Cain is not now sane."

Judge Bodey formally approved Dr. Gardner's certificate and promptly signed the necessary orders directing the Sheriff to convey the Defendant to Lima State Hospital for observation and evaluation for a period not to exceed one month, after which period he was to be returned to the court for sentencing. Judge Bodey had one final admonition for the sheriff. "In view of the events of this morning, the Court will expect you and your officers to take all those precautions which you deem necessary to keep the Defendant safely in custody."

The necessary paperwork was completed by four o'clock, and one half hour later, Cain was en route to Lima. As soon as the traveling party, consisting of Sheriff Miller, two deputies and Rollin Cain, had left the Troy city limits, Cain's demeanor brightened and he carried on a friendly conversation with the officers. They later reported that he seemed more normal than at any time since his surrender.

8

On May 25, precisely thirty days after his commitment to Lima State Hospital for observation, Rollin Cain was returned to Miami County for further proceedings. Along with the Defendant came a formal statement, addressed to the Court and signed by Dr. R. E. Bushong, superintendent of the hospital, advising that, in the opinion of the medical board of the hospital, the Defendant was sane.

Two days later, on May 27, 1935, Cain appeared in Judge Bodey's court, along with his counsel, Frank and Stanley Goodrich, as well as counsel for the State, Paul Klapp and Harley Enyeart. Judge Bodey acknowledged that the Lima State report had been received and filed with the Clerk, and the same was admitted into evidence by agreement of the parties and their respective counsel. Upon the basis of the Lima State report, he made a judicial finding that the Defendant was indeed sane, and that there was no reason why sentence should not be then imposed.

The sentencing order, after a preliminary recitation, provided that:

> *And the Defendant being inquired of whether or not he had anything to say why sentence should not now be passed against him, and the Defendant having made his statement, and Counsel appearing for him having made statements on his behalf, and the Court finding there is now no good or sufficient reason why the Court should not proceed to the passage of sentence:*
>
> *It is, therefore, ordered, adjudged and decreed by the Court that the Defendant Rollin Cain be committed to and confined in the Ohio State Penitentiary at Columbus, Ohio for the period of his life at hard labor, but without solitary confinement, and that he pay the costs of this prosecution taxed at $361.07, for which execution is ordered. And the Defendant is remanded to the custody of the sheriff for the execution of this sentence.*

Cain accepted his life sentence with surprising aplomb and calmly lit and smoked a cigarette in company with his counsel and with the deputies before being returned to the county jail. He was taken to the penitentiary by Sheriff Miller and two deputies that same afternoon.

"What a waste," lamented Paul Klapp to Harley Enyeart after it was over and Cain was in transit to the Ohio State Penitentiary. "What a tragic waste."

The two prosecutors were in Klapp's office at the end of the day, engaged in the tedious work of gathering, separating and ordering their separate files for storage. Enyeart looked at his colleague askance and queried, "A waste? What waste is that? Paul, we've just won the State's case, achieved a measure of justice for the victim and closure for her family. Where's the waste?

"I can understand that we'd both have been upset if we'd lost the case—or if we'd had to accept a conviction for manslaughter. But neither of those things happened. This was a clear and unequivocal win. We've worked very hard on the case, prepared well and presented it in the best tradition of our profession. I personally think we should be congratulating ourselves, celebrating our victory and all that that victory entails—justice, closure and, most importantly, vindication of our system of laws."

Paul Klapp shrugged. "I'm sure you're right about all of those things," he conceded. "We did our job well and got all that we'd asked for—but I just can't make myself feel all that good about it."

"That's obvious," said Enyeart. "You seem almost disconsolate over our having accomplished all that we set out to do, and I'm damned if I understand your reaction. Nor do I understand what sort of waste you're referring to."

Paul Klapp set aside the file folder he'd been fiddling with, picked up the glass he'd been nursing and sat back in his swivel chair. "You're right, Harley," he said. "I am disconsolate—not about the trial itself—we did that well, and I'm quite satisfied with the result. I'm just feeling depressed over the whole scenario. The waste. The tragic, needless and virtually inexplicable death of an innocent young girl, the appalling anguish occasioned both families, the Carmeans and the Cains, and even the total destruction of Rollin Cain's own chance of living a satisfying and meaningful life. In one quick, totally irrational act, so much was irretrievably lost to so many—and all for no good reason."

Attorneys (left to right) Robert S. Miller, Harley D. Enyeart, Judge Paul T. Klapp, Attorneys J. Cameron Dungan and Carl B. Felger.

He shook his head and repeated, "It just seems such a tragic waste."

Harley Enyeart nodded in agreement. "I hadn't really thought of it in that context. Of course you're right. I console myself with the fact that you and I had nothing to do with the Defendant's act of shooting his sweetheart, which, of course, set the whole thing in motion. Our part in the affair was only that of a clean-up operation."

Paul Klapp grimaced briefly, repossessed himself of the file he'd set aside and proceeded with putting it in order. "I suppose I need to accept the fact that it's not a perfect world and it's not populated by perfect people. Rollin Cain was a flawed personality and he did do a hell of a lot of damage. At least, we've prevented him from inflicting any more harm—for the nonce."

"And the 'flawed', much like the poor, we shall have with us forever," intoned Enyeart as if in benediction.

EPILOGUE

Rollin Cain was received at the Ohio State Penitentiary on May 27, 1935, and was transferred to the London Prison Farm on July 28, 1939. He was released on parole on July 30, 1945, and returned to Tipp City. He died there on March 14, 1946, as a result of an overdose of sleeping pills; his death was ruled a suicide.

ACKNOWLEDGMENTS

I think that I have previously gone on record with a promise that I was finished with this nonsense, i.e. that of attempting to reprise the events, and the subsequent trials, of the several murder cases which have captured the attention of Miami County's judicial system—as well as that of the general public—over the past century and a half. That commitment was made in consideration of the fact that no such cases had occurred to me. It thereafter dawned on me that there were, indeed, additional intriguing and noteworthy murder cases which were entitled to inclusion in my growing anthology. Of the three cases discussed in this latest effort, I cannot imagine how it was possible for me to have overlooked either Eddie McMullen or Cecile Huggins because I had personally witnessed parts of both trials and was well acquainted with virtually all of the participants, most especially the attorneys. Bill Harrelson was my law partner for 14 years until his death in 1985; shortly after my admission to practice I began a five-or-six-year term as an assistant prosecutor for Jim DeWeese; and I've tried both criminal and civil cases with Bill Dixon, Bill Thornburgh, Howard Swinehart, Bill Kessler, Ellis Kerr and Harley Enyeart. Although none of these lawyers are still practicing, each of them has, over the course of their long careers at the bar, demonstrated the highest degree of proficiency and professionalism.

As for the Rollin Cain case, I confess that I was totally unaware of it and only stumbled onto it in the course of my noodling about in the archives of the courthouse and the Miami County Historical Society. The so-called 'Kiss Killer' case intrigued me immensely and virtually demanded inclusion as one of the more bizarre, outré judicial events of the twentieth century.

As these several cases came, one way or another, to my attention, and at NJ's urging, I have felt fully justified in reneging on my ill-advised promise to cease and desist from the further examination and presentation of those cases from our local history which I have deemed to be both interesting and noteworthy. And, were these considerations insufficient to the purpose, I will also admit that I have consistently enjoyed the exercise.

Finally, I should like to acknowledge the contributions of some of the people who have provided valuable and much-needed assistance to me in the course of reconstruction of the events and the personae of the participants. I have previously mentioned the Honorable William E. Kessler, Eleanor Barringer, and both Bill and Pat Leffel, all of whom richly merit a reiteration of my appreciation for their interest in my project and for their sharing information which would have been otherwise inaccessible to me.

And, as always, I am once again indebted to Miami County Historical & Genealogical Society's Archivist Patrick Kennedy, and his assistant Barbara Besecker, both of whom were most helpful in the locating of a wide number of isolated and obscure factual matters—as was Linda Miller, one of the probate specialists in my own office. My personal secretary, Carolyn Benzies, has provided more assistance than I can possibly describe—most especially in converting my efforts to the printed page and resolving the persistent difficulties which routinely manifest themselves in my private, undeclared war with my own computer.

I deeply appreciate the several efforts of all of those persons specifically mentioned, along with the occasional and casual assistance of others too numerous to mention—and I hope you know who you are.

J.E.F.

ABOUT THE AUTHOR

John Fulker, like most attorneys, is an inveterate story-teller. Perhaps as an innocuous hobby, but most certainly as an obsession, he has spent much of his leisure time, over the past thirty years, in researching and reproducing in novelized format, the circumstances and the subsequent legal proceedings involved in a number of the more bizarre, outré and/or high-profile murder cases which have occurred and played out in his own Miami County, Ohio, over the entire course of its existence.

The senior partner of the Troy law firm of Faust, Harrelson, Fulker, McCarthy and Schlemmer, and presently in his sixtieth year of active legal practice, Fulker has previously authored four books, constituting an eight-piece anthology concerning such cases, all of which have been carefully selected because of the unique character of the crime itself, the participants, the extraordinary media attention accorded, the singular events of the ensuing trials—or some other nuance by which the cases were distinguished from the humdrum of our American judicial system.